GRACE
UNDER
PRESSURE

PENELOPE J. STOKES

NAVPRESS
A MINISTRY OF THE NAVIGATORS
P.O. BOX 6000, COLORADO SPRINGS, COLORADO 80934

The Navigators is an international Christian organi-
zation. Jesus Christ gave His followers the Great
Commission to go and make disciples (Matthew
28:19). The aim of The Navigators is to help fulfill
that commission by multiplying laborers for
Christ in every nation.

NavPress is the publishing ministry of The Navigators. NavPress publications are tools to help
Christians grow. Although publications alone
cannot make disciples or change lives, they can
help believers learn biblical discipleship, and
apply what they learn to their lives and ministries.

© 1990 by Penelope J. Stokes
All rights reserved, including translation
Library of Congress Catalog Card Number:
  89-63427
ISBN 08910-92870

Some of the anecdotal illustrations in this book
are true to life and are included with the permission of the persons involved. All other illustrations are composites of real situations, and any
resemblance to people living or dead is
coincidental.

Unless otherwise identified, Scripture quotations
in this publication are from the *Holy Bible: New
International Version* (NIV). Copyright © 1973,
1978, 1984, International Bible Society. Used by
permission of Zondervan Bible Publishers. Other
versions quoted are the *King James Version* (KJV);
and the *New American Standard Bible* (NASB),
© The Lockman Foundation 1960, 1962, 1963,
1968, 1971, 1972, 1973, 1975, 1977.

Printed in the United States of America

Contents

To Charette,
who has taught me more grace
than she knows.

Author

Penelope J. Stokes, Ph.D., professor of writing and literature for twelve years, left college teaching in 1985 to pursue full-time freelance writing and editing.

Nurtured in her Christian faith by the Navigators ministry, Dr. Stokes has been active in Bible teaching and discipling for many years. Her writing has appeared in several Christian magazines, and she has four books to her credit, including the recent Bible study, *Words in Season: Scripture Memory Tools* (World Wide Publications, 1988).

Acknowledgments

Many people have played important roles in the development and completion of this book.

Tom and Betty Tyndall gave me my first real taste of grace; although they were not present to see the culmination in this book, they share in its inception. Paul and Mary Jo Taintor walked with me through my dark night of the soul and pointed me toward the Light of grace. My friends have taught me lessons in grace that I could never have learned without them.

Special thanks are due to the members of my critique group: Charette Barta, Father Jerry Foley, Lois Walfrid Johnson, and Terry White. Excellent writers and thinkers, these

9

four friends have built me up and brought me down, encouraged me, corrected me, prayed for me, and supported me. Without them this work would not have been possible.

CHAPTER ONE

Finding Focus

*Grace is love that cares and stoops
and rescues.*
JOHN R. W. STOTT

C. S. Lewis, in his Space Trilogy, identifies Earth as the Bent Planet, ruled over by the Bent One. As Christians, our lives are profoundly influenced by the "bentness" of our environment: the fallenness that results in sin and sickness and pain for all of us.

Despite the inevitability of hurt and struggle in this wounded world of ours, Christians have tried to escape, ignore, or wish away the pain. But the pain does not go away. We still struggle with relationships, finances, emotional and physical illness, doubt, misunderstanding, failure, and fear.

In attempting to deny the reality of suffering and wish

ourselves into a life free from pain, Christians have also largely ignored the biblical mandate for dealing with struggles. Rather than casting ourselves upon the Lord who cares for us, we have developed an elaborate theology of performance. We have bought into the Bent One's lie: If only we *do enough*, if only we are *good enough*, somehow we can lift ourselves into God's pleasure and thus free ourselves from pain. The temptation to be like God is as strong as it ever was.

The bad news is that the problems remain. The struggle inherent in life doesn't go away when we close our eyes; we simply don't see the blow until it knocks us down. Then, dazed and confused, we wonder what hit us, we wonder where God is, we wonder what went wrong.

The Apostle Paul saw a similar problem among the Galatians: "You foolish Galatians!" he reproved them. "Who has bewitched you? . . . After beginning with the Spirit, are you now trying to attain your goal by human effort? Have you suffered so much for nothing . . . ?" (Galatians 3:1,3-4). Paul, an expert in the futility of legalism, recognized the necessity of grace—not just for initial salvation, but for the ongoing challenge of living out the life of Christ.

BEYOND SALVATION

The woman wept profusely as she told her story to a spellbound audience: her only child, a nine-year-old daughter, had been crushed beyond recognition in a construction accident. "I knew I had to get my life right with God. I had slipped away from Him, and that's why Lisa was nearly killed."

After a detailed account of her daughter's lengthy hospitalization, punctuated at points of crisis by the doctor's pronouncements of doom, the woman's tale began its upward turn. "But I got my life together," she declared. "I quit drinking, went back to church, and spent several hours a day in prayer and Bible study. And the Lord honored it—my daughter was miraculously healed and restored."

I have no doubt that the Lord did, indeed, lovingly intervene with His grace to rescue the woman's child. And the mother's prayer, Bible study, and lifestyle changes were, in and of themselves, positive. But the woman saw the Lord's action on her daughter's behalf as a result of her religious performance. She truly believed that if she had not reformed, her daughter would have died.

This well-meaning woman believed a fallacy held by many Christians. We receive salvation as a free gift of God's grace. But then we go on to live as if everything in life depended upon us—we act as if our faithfulness, our religious routines, and our good behavior are necessary to prime the pump of God's loving response. If we're good enough, spiritual enough, God will bless us. If not—well, we're out of luck.

Faithfulness, spiritual discipline, attention to the Word and prayer, and obedience to the commands of Scripture are, certainly, important aspects of our lives in Christ. But these actions, the changes we try to make in our behavior and attitudes, are intended to be *responses* to our awareness of the overwhelming, all-encompassing grace of a loving God. Too often we perceive them instead as *rituals* we can use to prod the Lord into action.

For many years, I operated under the same premise: God requires certain behaviors of me. If I do X, then He is obligated to respond with Y. Since He values time spent with Him, He obviously should allow me to pass my final exams even though my preparation time was spent studying the Bible rather than algebra. Since God places a high priority on prayer, He should bless my relationship with my family when I pray *for* them rather than communicate *with* them.

The absurdity of that logic became clear as I took a more objective look at the Scriptures. Jesus' ministry to people was not based on their goodness, any more than His sacrificial death was based on their acceptance of Him. If His grace had been offered first to the religiously righteous, the Pharisees would have been well-established in His Kingdom. But Jesus reached to the sinner, the prostitute, the thief, the fisherman, the poor widow—all people who had nothing to offer Him except themselves. And He taught His disciples to offer all they had to those who had no hope of repayment.

God's grace operates in the same fashion today—not just for salvation, but for all of life. He offers the inconceivable to the unworthy and withholds the expected from the deserving. Faith is not a system of proving our worthiness to Him, but the unadorned reception of what He offers, focusing not on the strength of the receiver, but on the character of the Giver.

BEYOND SELF

One afternoon many years ago, when I was teaching in a small Christian college, a young man named Alex appeared in my office doorway. Alex, a good student, prided himself on his classwork, but he had failed to turn in his final paper. Now, three days later, he awaited judgment.

"Well, Alex," I said as I looked over the paper he handed me. "Do you want grace or justice?"

"Better give me justice," he mumbled sheepishly, staring at his shoes. "I don't deserve grace."

At the time I chuckled inwardly at Alex's ironic statement, but in the intervening years I've come to realize that many Christians resist God's grace for precisely the same reason—because they feel they don't deserve it.

None of us "deserves" God's grace. At our worst, we are reprobate sinners, rebelling against the Lord's purposes in our lives. At our best, we stumble and fall, and our lives seem to be a continual cycle of sin and repentance, confession and absolution. Like Alex, when we are most aware of our shortcomings, we are also painfully aware of our undeserving.

Yet it is our very undeserving that places us in a position to receive grace. For grace is dependent not on our character, but on the character of God. "The LORD longs to be gracious to you," Isaiah 30:18 says; yet we hang our heads and cannot bring ourselves to look up into His loving face.

Jesus ministered His grace to those who best knew their need for Him—the leper, the outcast, the blind, the oppressed, the destitute. His loving acceptance of those who came to Him was never an excuse for sin. He simply embraced them, and in His embrace they found healing, release from bondage, and freedom to live in His example of love.

Only one group of people in the New Testament found themselves hindered from receiving the grace of God in Christ Jesus—the Pharisees, who were already confident of their acceptability to God. Revelation 3:17 reveals such false confidence for what it is: "You say, 'I am rich; I have acquired wealth and do not need a thing.' But you do not realize that you are wretched, pitiful, poor, blind and naked."

C. S. Lewis, in *The Great Divorce*, emphasizes the need to accept the grace of God. On the outskirts of Heaven, a character called the Big Ghost meets a man he knew in life—a convicted murderer who has been redeemed. "I gone straight all my life," the Big Ghost protests when he is confronted with his need for grace. "I done my best by everyone. . . . I'm not asking for anybody's bleeding charity."

"Then do, at once," the murderer responds. "Ask for the Bleeding Charity. Everything here is for the asking and nothing can be bought."[1]

When we realize that we are, apart from God's grace, "wretched, pitiful, poor, blind and naked," we acknowledge ourselves as desperate people—desperate enough to reach out and accept what we have not earned. We must reach out in that desperation in order to be saved; but that same desperation, that same need for the "Bleeding Charity," extends throughout our lives, in every circumstance we face.

Nothing of ourselves is sufficient to earn God's grace—neither the false confidence of the Pharisee nor the equally false pseudo-humility that declares, "Not me—I don't deserve it." Both attitudes center on self, and both keep us from embracing and accepting the grace offered to us by our Lord.

AN ISSUE OF FOCUS

Four workmen, all bricklayers, were working together on the same job. The hot, humid August afternoon was taking its toll, but each of the four worked on. "What are you doing?" asked an observer.

"I'm sweating it out for five bucks an hour," growled the first.

"I'm laying bricks," the second replied, and plopped a trowel full of mortar onto the top row.

The third workman was a bit more cheerful. "I'm building a wall," he said, standing back to admire his handiwork.

The fourth man straightened up from his wheelbarrow

full of mortar and mopped his face with a handkerchief. His eyes were glowing with excitement, and despite the heat he moved with enthusiasm, whistling as he put each brick in place. "I'm building a beautiful cathedral," he said. "See? Over there will be the great nave with its vaulted ceilings and stained glass windows, and people everywhere will come here to worship and bask in the glory of God."

Much of what happens in our lives depends upon perspective. If we acknowledge that life is difficult and conflicts are inevitable, if we recognize our own sin nature and the neediness of our souls, we come face to face with a very important question: "How can I discover and accept God's grace in the midst of the struggle?"

When we look at the world around us and within ourselves at our own fallibility, we have a choice. We can respond to what happens in our lives according to *circumstance* or according to *conviction*. When we evaluate God's goodness on the basis of circumstance, we inevitably vacillate in our understanding of His nature. Limited in knowledge and insight, we cry, "Why, God? If You love me, and if You're good, why did this happen to me?"

When we evaluate God's nature in light of the biblical revelation of His character, however, we respond differently. We develop a conviction of His faithfulness that cannot be swayed by the winds of circumstance. In difficulty and hardship, we then find ourselves able to say, "Lord, I know You love me. I know You're good. I don't understand, but I choose to trust You."

Peter experienced this distinction in a very tangible way. When Jesus said, "Come," Peter stepped out of the boat and began to walk on the water. As long as Peter kept his eyes on the Lord, he stayed above the waves. But halfway there, he thought about the impossibility of what he was doing. He looked around at the storm, felt the wind, saw the waves shifting beneath his feet, and became justifiably terrified. And he began to sink. (See Matthew 14:25-32.)

Like Peter, we face storms in our lives that threaten to destroy us. Jesus says, "Come, trust Me; walk through this with Me." The storm still rages, and the winds still howl, but we can do it—if we keep our attention fixed on the Source of grace and power.

The choice to trust God in the midst of difficult and confusing circumstances is made possible only through God's grace. And as we choose to shift our focus from the circumstances that threaten to sink us to the purposes of God, we see increasing measures of God's grace poured out in our lives.

When we struggle with persistent sin, God's forgiving grace restores us and sets us on the path again. When we face hardship or suffering, God's grace meets us in the midst of the pain, sharing it with us and teaching us through it. When we are subject to the Lord's discipline, His grace purifies us and makes us whole. When we come into a crisis of forgiveness, He reminds us of His forgiveness for us and enables us to forgive others and grow in compassion.

In every difficult circumstance, God's grace reaches down—not necessarily to change the circumstances and make us comfortable, but to change us and make us strong and loving. Too often we Christians are shortsighted when we look at the seemingly overwhelming problems in our lives. We want a God who makes it all better, relieving us of the stress of the moment and the necessity for change. We want a God who gets us out of the fix we are in.

Our God, however, is much more gracious than that. He looks at the long-term effects of our difficulties and pain. He sees beyond the immediate trouble to the growth and Christlikeness that can come out of our conflicts. The God of all grace is able to take the worst of situations and use it to the best advantage in the lives of those He loves.

The good news is that the Good News hasn't changed: Immanuel, God with us, is still with us. His grace, sufficient to redeem us when we could not redeem ourselves, is equally sufficient to meet our present needs. God wants to infuse His grace into every circumstance of our lives.

We need to learn to perceive and live daily in the grace of God. We do not hear grace whisper to us that, no matter how dark the present trial, our God is equal to it. We have misdirected our focus, and so we see only the chaos around us and hear only the voices that shout to us of hopelessness and despair.

Too often we look through a close-up lens, seeing the minute detail of the present circumstance, while everything else around us blurs into oblivion. We see the aphid on the leaf and miss the fragile beauty of the rose. Sometimes we need to change lenses, to gaze at the distance through the telephoto of His grace, to focus our attention once more upon the One who says, "My grace is sufficient for you, for my power is made perfect in weakness" (2 Corinthians 12:9).

Redirecting our focus to look up at His grace does not always make our difficulties disappear or smooth the uneven paths. Sometimes God intervenes with His power to improve our circumstances; more often He intervenes with His grace to deepen our characters. But once we learn to attune our ears to His voice through the clamor, we gain a perspective on our circumstances that we have never had before.

Through an understanding of God's grace, we can look beyond the setbacks of daily life and see that there is a higher purpose, a deeper reality to our experience. Our pain is not wasted; our Gethsemane nights do not go unnoticed. God is there, offering His grace and seeking to reveal

Himself more fully to us. As we listen to the word of grace His Spirit speaks, we can see Him—and ourselves—more clearly.

As we learn to live in that grace, we also learn to extend it to others, offering comfort and hope, reaching out with grace-filled, loving touches to help and support those around us.

Christians have lived too long in condemnation, in criticism, in the frustration of futile self-effort. We labor so hard and accomplish so little. In the midst of our noisy struggles, the Spirit speaks a quiet word of grace:

"Be.
Be still.
Be still and know.
Be still and know that I am.
Be still and know that I am God."

The message of Psalm 46:10 is, "Cease striving, let go, relax, and know that I am God." God reigns; He is God, so we don't have to be. We don't have to have a five-step ritual for getting our prayers answered. We don't need to see all the possibilities or know all the answers. We don't have to deserve His grace. God is our Creator. He is just, He is faithful. He offers stability and growth amid confusion and death. He has the future—as well as the present and the past—under control.

As we rest upon God's character, depending on the truth of who He is, we can wait in hope for His grace to be revealed. Whatever the circumstances, whatever God does or does not do, we can be certain of His grace extended to us. We can change our focus, looking not at what is visible, but at the eternal truth of the invisible. We can transfer our gaze from God's hand to His face.

CHAPTER TWO

The Grace of Discipline

*As sure as God puts his children in the
furnace he will be in the furnace
with them.*
CHARLES H. SPURGEON

M y niece Martha was only four—but old enough to know better—the morning I stayed with her awaiting the arrival of her grandparents. I was clearing the breakfast dishes, when out of the corner of my eye I caught a glimpse of movement at the table.

I turned just in time to see the child raise her glass of orange juice, hold it at arm's length over the carpet, and deliberately, premeditatedly, drop it. Then she smiled at me with an elfin gleam in her eye and folded her little hands on the tray of her high chair.

When the grandparents arrived, Martha was confined to her room. Dashing through the hall into the living room, she flung herself at her grandfather—my father—and wailed, "Pa Jim! Pa Jim! Aunt Penny spanked me!"

"Oh, did she now?" my father responded, trying to hide his amusement.

"Yeah!" Martha proclaimed. "And you know what? I deserved it!"

My brother's little daughter, at age four, perceived a truth that many of us as adults tend to forget: Although discipline is difficult to receive, we deserve it. We *need* to be corrected so that we can grow. And like our earthly parents, our heavenly Parent provides, if not always what we deserve, precisely what we *need.* God uses the circumstances of our lives to discipline us, to correct our course, to refine our character, to mold us into the image of Jesus Christ.

A MATTER OF LIFE AND DEATH

Dan, a young Christian zealous in the newness of his faith and convinced that the Lord had taught him all he needed to know, began subtly to resist the instruction of his pastor. He didn't want to take the time to be trained, he just wanted to lead others to the Lord! When his pastor gently reproved the boy about his know-it-all attitudes, Dan replied, "Ah, c'mon, why can't you just let me do my own thing? It's not a matter of life and death, y'know!"

But the Lord's discipline *is* a matter of life and death: "These commands are a lamp, this teaching is a light, and the corrections of discipline are the way to life" (Proverbs 6:23). The book of Proverbs abounds with such warnings: "He will die for lack of discipline" (5:23); "Whoever finds [wisdom] finds life and receives favor from the LORD. But . . . all who hate [wisdom] love death" (8:35-36); "He who heeds discipline shows the way to life, but whoever ignores correction leads others astray" (10:17).

During my teenage years I ignored correction, resisting the wooing of the Holy Spirit as He called me to follow Christ. I was rebellious and insecure, and more than anything, I feared that God would force me to change and admit that I had been wrong. I didn't want to be disciplined.

In my twentieth year, that rebellion almost led to my death. I teetered on the precipice of suicide. Finally I chose to live and flung myself, not from the roof of the college dormitory, but into the arms of a waiting Savior.

The life-and-death choices we make in response to God's correction and discipline are not always so dramatic. In later years, as I struggled—with varying degrees of success—to be obedient to the Lord and responsive to His voice, other experiences demanded that I choose life on a daily basis by choosing to embrace the changes God wanted to work in my life.

THE LOVE MOTIVE

Many of us have a problem embracing God's discipline and perceiving it as grace rather than punishment. Some people have grown up in a household where no disciplinary boundaries were imposed at all. Others have endured physical and emotional abuse in the name of discipline. In either case, a clear, balanced perspective of God's loving correction may be hard to come by.

Whatever our personal experiences of human discipline, the Bible provides irrefutable evidence of the Lord's motives in bringing us to discipline: *"Those whom I love I rebuke and discipline.* So be earnest, and repent" (Revelation 3:19, emphasis added). God is moved by love to correct us, so that we might become like Jesus Christ. His correction results in *blessedness* (Job 5:17), *righteousness* (Hebrews 12:11), *knowledge* (Proverbs 1:7), *wisdom* (Proverbs 29:15), and *life* (Proverbs 10:17).

Even after we accept intellectually that God's discipline is designed for our good, not as punishment for sin, we may still have a difficult time embracing discipline as a demonstration of God's grace. Even Jesus, who did not sin, learned obedience to the Father through the discipline process of suffering (Hebrews 5:8). We who seek to follow Him must take the same path.

The terms used in Scripture for the process of becoming like Christ help us to form a positive concept of God's work in our lives. *Discipline* implies ongoing training—learning to be a disciple. *Correction* is an adjustment in direction. *Purifying* and *refining*—as gold and silver are refined by fire—evoke images of the crucible: The heat may seem destructive as it melts down the ore, but after the process is complete, a costly ingot is the result. The concept of *chastening* can be traced to the same Latin source as the word *chaste*, or pure—God's chastening results in purity.

The central principle, then, of the biblical perspective of discipline appears in Hebrews 12:11: "No discipline seems pleasant at the time, but painful. Later on, however, it produces a harvest of righteousness and peace for those who have been trained by it."

CHANNELS OF GOD'S DISCIPLINE

Hal's frustration showed on his face as he tried to sort out the circumstances of his life. "I was taught," he said, "that difficulty in a Christian's life comes from Satan. So when my car breaks down, or I'm short of cash at the end of the month, or my wife and I have a fight, I rebuke the Devil." He paused and scratched his head. "But it just doesn't seem to be working," he said. "If the Devil is the source of all this trouble, why won't he leave me alone?"

Hal was discovering—much to his dismay—that there are many reasons for difficulty and struggle in the Christian life. Some of our battles may be direct warfare with a very real Enemy, of course—our struggles may be linked to individual encounters with Satanic forces. But many other obstacles that we face are simply the normal issues of human life. How, then, can we know when God is trying to get our attention to discipline us?

The Lord's correction comes to us through a variety of channels and experiences. But in general, we can conclude that *discipline is God's use of suffering or persecution in our lives to correct and instruct us and to develop more completely in us the image of Jesus Christ.* Such discipline can be a whispered warning that I should be more gentle with a hurting friend or a major life change that brings me back to biblical priorities.

Revelation comes into our lives in three ways: *Scripture, other people,* and *circumstances.* Because of human error and our tendency toward rationalization, each vehicle of revelation has inherent dangers that need to be avoided. None is flawless or absolute, but all are important avenues to spiritual growth.

Scripture is the most direct method by which God disciplines and corrects us. "All Scripture," Paul told Timothy, "is God-breathed and is useful for teaching, rebuking, correcting and training in righteousness, so that the man of God may be thoroughly equipped for every good work" (2 Timothy 3:16-17).

When we read the Bible and discover principles of godliness, or when the Holy Spirit reminds us of those principles, we also discover that our own attitudes and lifestyles may run counter to the biblical norm. Then we have a choice: to refuse the correction and stubbornly maintain the status quo, or to open ourselves to the Holy Spirit's working, tell the Lord we are willing to change, and look for ways to incorporate the change into our lives.

The Bible is an invaluable source of correction for us, and often one of the means God uses to direct changes in our lives. Yet we need to be aware that the Bible is not the *only* channel by which God disciplines His people. I remember a country gospel song from my youth that proclaims, "Me and Jesus, we got our own thing goin'; we don't need anybody to tell us what it's all about."

It's a deceptive half-truth: We *do* need other people to "tell us what it's all about," to give us an objective view of our lives, and to help interpret Scripture and the circumstances surrounding God's work in our lives. We need to take care not to fall into the "me and Jesus" fallacy.

People are also an important vehicle of God's purifying work—whether they are aware of it or not. Most of the problems in our lives center around relationships, and much of God's refining comes through those very relationships. The word of correction may come through a pastor's sermon, through the prophetic voice of a spiritual mentor, or through the angry words of a neglected spouse. But however it comes, when we find ourselves challenged by the words or actions of another, we need to evaluate that challenge, sifting through it for the truth God may be speaking to us.

It is, without doubt, easier to receive and embrace correction when it is offered in a loving and constructive way. Even when challenges or criticism come harshly, on the unsheathed barbs of resentment and hostility, we still need to discover the truth about ourselves and allow God to change us.

"Open rebuke is better than secret love. Faithful are the

wounds of a friend," Proverbs 27:5-6 (KJV) declares; and Ecclesiastes 7:5 says, "It is better to heed a wise man's rebuke than to listen to the song of fools."

Often the "song of fools" comes through my own lips, ringing in my ears the refrain of rationalization. I don't want to change. My self-esteem is tied up in maintaining my present position; therefore I refuse to hear the voice of the Lord when it comes through a source I prefer not to recognize. I need to listen to those who bring rebuke and to respond, "Blessed is he who comes in the name of the LORD" (Psalm 118:26).

On the other side of the coin, of course, is the importance of maintaining balance when I am used as a mouthpiece for the word of correction to come to someone else. The Bible is filled with instructions to the corrector: "If your brother sins, rebuke him" (Luke 17:3); "Those who sin are to be rebuked publicly, so that the others may take warning" (1 Timothy 5:20); "Preach the Word . . . correct, rebuke and encourage—with great patience and careful instruction" (2 Timothy 4:2); "Rebuke them sharply, so that they will be sound in the faith" (Titus 1:13).

Lest we leap too readily into the role of corrector, we need to realize that in most of these situations established spiritual authority was involved: both Timothy and Titus were recognized pastors. There are others who have such authority, certainly—teachers, parents, counselors, disciplemakers. But we need to be very careful, when we speak correction to others, that we do not seek to manipulate or control. Even when we are used as tools in His hand, God is the One responsible for adjustments in other people's lives.

Circumstance is an avenue of discipline that many of us struggle with, yet can't seem to escape. Even when we try to "do right," things seem to go wrong: we wreck the car, over-water the ferns, over-commit our schedules, overdraw the checkbook, forget a lunch date, ignore the children. If we are willing to face ourselves squarely and allow the Lord to shine the piercing ray of His grace into our life circumstances, we can grow—not beyond our troubles, but in the midst of them.

"Life is difficult," says psychologist M. Scott Peck in *The Road Less Traveled*.[1] It will always be difficult in this world, and those very difficulties may prove to be God's best chisels to chip away the rough edges of our personalities.

The conflicts we face stem from two basic sources: original sin and individual sin. Because of original sin, we live in a fallen world—a world of injustices where teenagers lose their lives to drugs and accidents and suicide. We grapple daily with the results of Adam and Eve's disobedience—incurable disease, problem relationships, psychological dysfunction in the family, divorce, rebellion, walls that divide.

Our individual sin and resistance to the Spirit result in additional difficulties: my temper creates a barrier between myself and my friend; irresponsibility causes me to lose my job; pride keeps me from reconciling with my estranged parents.

Even when circumstances are good, they may be bad. Success and stability may lure us into a false sense of security, the deceptive feeling of having arrived at such a level of spiritual contentment that it's unnecessary to think about growing anymore.

The good news is that God's grace is at work in all these circumstances. He did not *cause* my neighbors' child to be hit by a car, but He can work in the midst of their grief. He did not ordain sickness, but He can use it to draw people to Himself.

Even individual sin is not lost to God's redeeming

power. He did not create me with a tendency to lie, nor does He condone it, but even in the midst of my sin, He can bring grace, opening my eyes to the source of my fault and my heart to His restoring power.

Nothing is wasted in the economy of grace. Everything that comes into my life—every relationship, every circumstance, every experience of joy or pain—can be used by God to teach me, to discipline and correct me, to refine the gold of my life and purify me for His glory. And from that perspective, I can learn to embrace, rather than despise, the discipline of the Lord.

DESPISING THE DISCIPLINE

"Do not despise the LORD's discipline," Proverbs 3:11-12 admonishes, "and do not resent his rebuke, because the LORD disciplines those he loves, as a father the son he delights in."

Our techniques for despising the Lord's correction are varied and subtle, but they all have the same result: They keep us from enjoying the fruit of righteousness that results when we are trained by the Spirit's discipline.

We complain, we blame, we ignore the lesson through pride, we avoid the prophets in our lives, we harbor bitterness toward those who bring the word of rebuke. Unlike my niece Martha, who knew she deserved it when she was corrected, many of us resist God's discipline as if it were some unusual or distasteful punishment brought about by a sadistic enemy. But our Lord is not our enemy, and He is no sadist. He delights, not in pain, but in progress. Yet He knows that the growing pains inherent in His chastening are often necessary to keep us close to Him.

Hebrews 12:15 offers a cryptic warning concerning the discipline of the Lord: "See to it that no one misses the grace of God and that no bitter root grows up to cause trouble and defile many." Often, especially when rebuke comes through a human source, we can miss the grace of God in that discipline—we can fail to see that this correction is not from a human source, but from a divine one. Defensive at being challenged, we quickly erect the walls of our spiritual fortresses, resist the correction, and nurture bitterness against the one who brought us face to face with our shortcomings.

The dust storm we raise by dragging our heels at the Lord's correction only blinds us to His purposes. Husband, wife, child, parent, pastor, church, Satan, or circumstances are not responsible for our battles. There are no accidents with God, no useless tears, no unrequited love; He uses everything to accomplish His purposes in us.

DRAW NEAR TO THE BURNING BUSH

"I want to receive God's discipline freely," Mari protested, "but why does it have to be so hard?" A businesswoman in her early thirties, Mari wanted to enjoy a settled, orderly life. "I just don't know how to handle all this chaos," she admitted. "It seems like every time a major spiritual change comes along, it's accompanied by a major emotional upheaval as well. Can't God speak to me someplace besides the wilderness?"

God can speak to us when we are surrounded by comfort and contentment, of course. But many Christians find that they hear God's voice and see His direction most clearly when they are in the wilderness—in a place of emotional, or even physical, isolation where fewer distractions vie for their attention.

Our wilderness experiences can be as simple as a two-hour walk in the woods or as uprooting as the loss of a job or a move across the country. We can enter emotional wildernesses as well: the breakup of an intimate relationship, the death of a loved one, depression following a major success or failure.

Most of us try to avoid the wilderness. We turn on the television, seek out a new romantic interest, or in extreme cases, drown our sorrows in addictions. Rarely do we enter the wilderness of our own accord, ready to hear what the Lord may say to us there.

We may have the mistaken notion that the wilderness is for losers—after all, the most striking example in Scripture of a wilderness experience is the journey of the children of Israel to the Promised Land. Because of their disobedience and rebellion, an eleven-day journey took forty years, and the Apostle Paul cites them as an excellent example of how not to live (1 Corinthians 10:1-13).

But before the Exodus began, Moses the patriarch, leader of the people, spent his own time in the wilderness. Partly because of circumstance and partly because of his own sin, Moses ran from the palaces of Egypt and escaped to the desert. There he tended sheep until the Lord spoke to him.

Through Moses' experience, we can gain insight and learn how to embrace the refining discipline of the Lord.

Enter the wilderness. Like Moses, we do not escape the discipline of the Lord by running. Whether we realize it or not, we are driven by the Spirit into the wilderness, just as Jesus entered His time of testing (Luke 4:1). Rather than avoiding that confrontation by filling our lives with activity, we need to be still and wait for the Lord to speak.

Observe, and draw near. In Exodus 3, as Moses went about the business of tending his father-in-law's sheep, he saw something unusual: a bush that burned but was not consumed. Often we feel that never-ending flame as the fire of God's Spirit refines our lives, calling us to obedience through conflict and inner struggle. God does not delight in the pain we experience, but He uses it to draw us to Himself and direct our attention to His purposes. And often, like that bush burning in the wilderness, the very issue that plagues us most will be the channel through which God speaks.

Take off your shoes. If we want to respond openly to God's correction, we must be willing to be vulnerable both to Him and to others. "No discipline seems pleasant at the time," the writer of Hebrews insists (12:11). Our feet burn on the desert sands and bleed against the rocks. But as the Lord speaks, we become less conscious of the heat and the pain and are caught up in the glory of His presence. The wilderness is holy ground.

Listen, and obey. The interchange between Moses and God in Exodus 3 reveals two separate agendas: God's and Moses'. God called Moses to be the deliverer of Israel. Moses thought Aaron was better qualified for the job. "Who am I, that I should go to Pharaoh and bring the Israelites out of Egypt?" Moses protested.

"I will be with you," God responded (Exodus 3:11-12).

Like Moses, we have our own ideas of what needs to be changed in our lives, of what direction we need to go. When God shows us what *He* wants to correct, we may feel entirely inadequate to the task—and rightly so. But God says to us, as He said to Moses, "I will be with you."

We can never change ourselves; we can never, in our own strength and wisdom, conform ourselves to the image of Christ. And God does not expect us to change. He asks us to cooperate with Him as His Spirit works within us.

The distinction is an important one: it is the difference

between law and grace, between self-righteousness and the righteousness of Christ, between personal improvement and spiritual growth. I cannot change myself; I have tried, and I know it does not work. But God's Spirit can change me; He can make me into the person He created me to be. He alone can overcome the results of the Fall in my life; He alone can remedy my private falls as well.

There is a higher reality than the circumstances we face, a deeper truth than despair. The good news of Jesus Christ is *grace*: No matter what our sin, no matter what our circumstances, God's grace can bring growth and change— and ultimately joy—out of the dark wildernesses of our lives. We have only to approach the burning bush, remove the shoes that protect us from pain, and surrender ourselves to the plans of a loving Father.

In a human sense, we do deserve discipline, as four-year-old Martha recognized. We are sinners, desperately in need of the correcting hand, the purifying fires, the Lord's chastening. If we are to take on the image of our Lord, serious adjustments need to be made.

But in a higher sense, we can never deserve God's correction. We cannot earn or deserve the freedom, the righteousness, the peace that come with the training and discipline of the Lord. We do not deserve the love that will not leave us to our own devices. Discipline is a gift of God's grace.

CHAPTER THREE

Failure: Turning the Curse into a Blessing

*God whispers in our pleasures
but shouts in our pain.*
C. S. LEWIS

D r. Frances Bolen, who reputedly ate first-year graduate students for breakfast, turned in her chair as I peered around the corner into her office. "Well, well," she chuckled softly. "And what can I do for you?"

My hands trembled as I laid the term paper on the desk in front of her. In the top left corner was a neat red *F*. "I . . . I came to talk about the grade on this paper."

"Did you ever get an F before?"

"No, ma'am."

"You used sources in your paper that are not documented. Do you know what that's called?" Her voice was gentle, as if she were instructing a preschooler.

"You mean plagiarism?"

"Exactly."

"Yes, but Dr. Bolen, I didn't mean to." I took a deep breath and grasped at a final straw of hope. "If I write this paper over, will you . . . ."

"The grade stands." She smiled wryly. "You'll be more careful next time, won't you?"

"Yes, ma'am." Realizing I was beaten, I headed for the door.

"Penny?"

"Yes?"

The professor raised her coffee cup in salute. "Failure is good for your soul."

Good for my soul! I thought at the time. *How can failure be good for me?* But in the years since that encounter, I have discovered that she was right.

THE UNIVERSAL TEST

"I'm a failure," John said simply—and he meant it. He was a major unit supervisor in his company, and he had just been offered a substantial raise and more responsibility. He was a leader in his church. He and his wife had a happy, productive marriage. But his son had been arrested at a party where drugs were being distributed. John had passed every "test of success" except the one most important to him.

Whether or not John was responsible for his son's misbehavior is not the question. He felt he had failed, and no other success in his life could make up for that failure.

The fact is, we could all claim to be experts in failure. A marriage warps and breaks; a business collapses into bankruptcy; a child runs away from home; a successful pastor falls into infidelity with a member of his congregation.

On a smaller scale, human beings struggle with hurt

feelings, hot tempers, ineffective methods of communication. Anne abuses her credit cards and goes deeply into debt; Ed forgets his daughter's birthday; Randy tries to control his girlfriend, and she drops him in favor of a more sensitive guy.

Many of the most memorable characters in Bible history are similarly marked by failure. They are not—in human terms—candidates for canonization. Moses was a murderer; Abraham a liar; David both a murderer and an adulterer. Peter denied his Lord, and Paul systematically executed the followers of Christ.

Scripture also provides examples of failure not related to sin. Joseph was a victim of his brothers' jealousy, and he endured exile and imprisonment because of them. Daniel, one of the brightest young men in Israel with an almost unlimited future ahead of him, was taken into slavery in Babylon.

Failure is a universal experience. We all fail—whether as victims of uncontrollable circumstance, or as a result of our own lack of wisdom. Whatever the cause of our failures, we need to learn how to understand them in the light of God's grace and allow Him to redeem them for our good, for His glory, and—ultimately—for usefulness in ministry.

FACING FAILURE

When Robert took over as vice president of the company, his colleagues all applauded him. He was bright, personable, and able to take control. But as the months went by, they began to see another side of Robert. Even in the smallest issues, he was unable to take advice or admit that he was wrong. The pressure mounted, and Robert's personality began to change—for the worse.

Robert's colleagues tried to help him understand that

he could relax, that he didn't have to be right all the time. But Robert was unable to listen to their counsel. He never learned to face up to his failings, and thus he was never able to allow God to work through them. Within a year he moved on to another job, leaving anger and bitterness in his wake.

Facing failure is never easy. Self-image and self-esteem are closely bound up in our performance. When we sin, make mistakes, or commit errors in judgment—even when we are victims of circumstance—we try to cover up rather than facing matters squarely. We want to save face, and so we try to convince ourselves and others that we are in the right.

Ironically, such self-justification never makes us feel better about ourselves. We fall into patterns of falsehood that actually hinder us from seeing and responding to God's grace. We can, however, take some practical steps to break those patterns and allow God's grace to transform our failings.

Tell the truth. "I know my transgressions, and my sin is always before me," David confessed in Psalm 51:3. He had committed adultery with Bathsheba and arranged for the death of her husband, Uriah. If we intend to confront our failures and let God work in them, we need to tell ourselves the truth about the failure like David did. Sometimes we sin, and we must acknowledge that before God. At other times we make honest mistakes or errors in judgment.

Many of us, however, have difficulty knowing the difference. We excuse outright sin far too casually, saying, "Ah, I'm only human." Yet we treat ordinary human error as if we expect perfection of ourselves: "I should have known better!"

We need to step back and see our failings in the light of God's Word, learning to determine the difference between sin and human failure. When we violate God's express standards of morality and integrity, we need to confess that as sin. When we've made an honest mistake, we need to forgive ourselves.

Accept responsibility. Recognizing our humanness, discerning between sin and honest error, in no way relieves us of the need to acknowledge our own responsibility. King David, when confronted by the prophet Nathan about his adultery, made no effort to excuse or justify himself. "I have sinned against the LORD," he responded (2 Samuel 12:13). David openly admitted his sin and repented, and his honest acceptance of his responsibility paved the way for his forgiveness and restoration.

Some of us, however, tend to take responsibility we should not shoulder. We take things personally; we try to "make things better," to please others, to keep the peace at any price.

A clear, honest evaluation of responsibility in such circumstances is often difficult. We tend toward one of two extremes: either to shoulder all the blame all the time, or to blame others for our difficulties. Facing up to ourselves, admitting our shortcomings, and evaluating our responsibility are essential elements in moving beyond failure into the grace God offers.

Look for God's control. Whether our failures are a result of our own sin or brought about by circumstance, God is still in control. He sees our hearts; He knows our needs; He is able to use every circumstance of our lives to enhance His image in us.

In human terms, the Apostle Paul began his Christian life in failure. He was a Pharisee, a legalist, a religious zealot. Believing himself to be absolutely in the right, he officiated at the stoning of Stephen and then set out to track down and execute the followers of Christ. But even before Paul's Damascus road conversion, God's grace was at work in his life and circumstances.

When Paul wrote to the Galatians, delivering to them the good news of grace in Christ, he pointed to his past—to his failures—as the evidence of God's work in him. He could speak with authority about God's grace, for he had firsthand knowledge of the destructiveness of legalism. God used Paul's past failures as a foundation of his present ministry.

Discover the principles. When I became a Christian, I was quickly thrust into positions of leadership. My natural talents and spiritual gifts served me well in that capacity, but certain faults in my personality led me into some resounding failures. I pushed too hard, demanded too much, expected growth too fast in those to whom I ministered. I manipulated, and I became a sheepdog rather than a shepherd. I failed. In several glaring instances, I drove people away from the Lord in my zeal to make them mature.

Seeing my failure, I wanted to abandon ministry altogether, to go away by myself so I wouldn't perpetuate the pattern. But after a time of withdrawal, the Lord began to make clear to me the fact that I didn't have to give up—I just needed to grow up. Over the years, I've begun to learn that ministry is God's work and disciples are God's people. He is responsible for them, not I.

With that recognition has come a remarkable freedom. I can take that knowledge and apply it to present relationships. I can carry the principle into the future and leave the experience of failure behind me.

If we are to grow through failure, we need to be able to leave our experiences of pain in the past, where they belong. God offers grace, forgiveness, a new start. He does not require us to prove that we'll do better next time; He merely reaches down to us, helps us up, shows us the lesson of our failure, and sends us forward.

Discern the character. When John described himself as a "failure" because his son was apprehended in a drug raid, he made an error common to many of us: he mistook *circumstance* for *character*. Even if I bring failure and heartache upon myself by deliberate sin, even if my life is marred by bad judgments and unwise decisions, I still need to discern between my actions and my character. It is fair and right and healthy to admit, "I have failed." But "I have failed" is a far different statement from "I am a failure." I believe that *failure* is a noun that should be applied to events or circumstances, not individuals.

In *Walking on Water*, Madeleine L'Engle discusses the concept of *naming*—the process by which we identify ourselves and one another. L'Engle's perspective on naming is a positive, creative one. "When we name each other," she says, "we are sharing in the joy and privilege of incarnation."[1] We become what we are named; we name others, and help to shape their image of themselves. But naming can also be a negative and destructive power.

When a father tells his daughter, "You're so stupid; can't you do anything right?" he names his child *Rejected*. When a mother says to her children, "I gave up everything for you, and you don't appreciate a thing I've done," she does, in L'Engle's words, "participate in their incarnation"— she gives birth to children named *Worthless* and *Burden*.

"I have failed" is a declaration of fact. When a relationship goes wrong, when plans fall through, when mistakes bring about hurt and mistrust, when financial security falters, I may have failed. But such failure is an event, a set of circumstances that can be dealt with and, ultimately, left behind.

To say "I am a failure" names me, locks me in, denies the possibility of growth. It is a statement of character: No matter where I go, no matter how much I learn or change or mature, that "failure" will always be with me, for I cannot escape myself.

One mother vividly demonstrated the difference between failure as a circumstance and failure as a statement of character. Her five-year-old son, bored with standing in line waiting to be seated in a restaurant, discovered the coat room and began swinging from the rod. When she caught a glimpse of her young Tarzan, she leveled a reproving gaze toward him and said, "Bad choice, Jason. Bad choice."

With that one well-chosen reprimand, the woman spoke volumes both to the boy's behavior and to his self-image. To make "bad choices" is not to be a "bad person." Because I fail does not mean I am a failure.

We can put ourselves in a position to receive the restoring grace of God in the midst of our failures. If we acknowledge failing as an experience rather than a personality characteristic, our self-esteem does not have to be tied up in an admission of failure. We can confront the problem honestly, take responsibility, learn and grow from our mistakes, and allow God's grace to meet us at the point of our insufficiency.

PINPOINTING PERFECTIONISM

"I have a terrible time accepting failure—or anything less than sheer perfection," Janice confessed. "I grew up with the Mothers' Motto ringing in my ears: *Anything worth doing is worth doing right!* Now, as an adult, everything I attempt has to be done perfectly, the one right way, or I think that it's not good enough."

Janice, like many of us, struggles with the problems of perfectionism, that "propensity for setting extremely high standards and being displeased with anything less."[2] Perfectionists are driven to perform, and their sense of value derives not simply from having attempted a worthy goal, or even from the accomplishment of it, but from the perfection of every detail.

Perfectionism, in the extreme, renders us unable to act at all. We fear failure, so we don't begin.

Perfectionism versus excellence. Wanting to fulfill our potential in Christ is, of course, not sin; Jesus Himself did all things well (Mark 7:37). But unbridled perfectionism is often a distortion of the "be perfect, as Christ is perfect" principle. Such a creed lands us in a pressure cooker of expectations. In perfectionism we have no freedom to fail. We give ourselves no room to grow, and there's nowhere to go but down.

A commitment to excellence, on the other hand, sets us free to aim high and entrust ourselves to God's grace, because we are also at liberty to miss the mark. If my wonderful idea for streamlining office procedure ends in chaos, if I initiate a relationship with someone who rejects me, or if I launch out into a new realm of ministry that does not succeed, my whole self-image does not hinge on that one failure. I can set my sights on excellence without having to be perfect.

Gordon MacDonald, in *Ordering Your Private World*, draws a distinction between the person who is *driven* and the one who is *called.* The driven person operates according to a "psychology of achievement" by which his worth and value are affirmed by his accomplishments. That is not grace. The called person, on the other hand, is motivated to excellence by stewardship, by commitment to Christ, by an acceptance of his abilities and purpose as the gift of God's grace. The outward manifestations may often look similar, but the inward motivation, and the resulting effect on the spirit, are vastly different.

Enough is enough. "Sometimes being at home with my wife and children is a higher spiritual priority than being at church every time the doors open," one friend confessed. "Playing Trivial Pursuit® with the family may not seem very spiritual, but I think on occasion it might please God more than leaving them at home so I can attend one more meeting."

For the Christian, the perfectionist compulsion often takes the form of religious overkill. One woman I know played the piano, kept the nursery, taught primaries, organized vacation Bible school, hosted small groups, led a women's circle, and volunteered time in the church office on weekdays. She was always appreciated, always applauded, and always exhausted.

When she finally recognized her compulsions, she began to weed out certain activities. "I felt like a good person, a valuable person, because I was always *doing*," she confessed. "Now I know I don't have to be superwoman—Christ accepts me for myself. It was time to say, 'Enough is enough.'"

Although perfectionists desperately need to appropriate the grace of God in their lives, they often resist grace because, for them, enough is *never* enough. Those first-century perfectionists, the Pharisees, prided themselves on keeping not only the Law, but all the manmade ordinances as well. They even thought to please God by tithing tiny portions of spices—dill, mint, cumin—so that the Law would be fulfilled down to its most detailed interpretation.

Then God, through the death and resurrection of Jesus, declared, "Enough is enough. Lay down your scorecards; this sacrifice is all you need."

Often our tendencies toward perfectionism make us unwilling or unable to accept the sufficiency of Christ. Somehow we think we should be capable of doing everything, of understanding everything, of making the right decisions, of controlling our own lives. Such a mindset was Lucifer's downfall, and it was the basis for his seduction of the human race into sin. Satan wanted to be equal with God; Adam and Eve wanted to "be like God." They wanted to rise above God's will for their lives and control their own destinies.

The Enemy's snare is just as subtle for us. We may not see it, but we fall into the same trap. When we expect perfection from ourselves, we find oursleves working to achieve righteousness.

We are, in the final analysis, human—flawed, struggling, gloriously human. Perfectionism is the belief— conscious or subconscious—that we should be flawless, like God. But the drive to be "like God" through perfectionism is a far cry from the desire to be godly. Our efforts will never bring us to the level of being "like God"; God's grace in Christ exalts us into godliness.

Perfectionism makes accepting and growing through failure especially difficult. But failure can, ironically, help set us free from the demands of perfectionism. Failure shows us our un-God-ness, our imperfection. Without excusing sin, we can look at ourselves and recognize that we are, indeed, human and not God. While we may aim toward excellence, we do not have to be shackled by unreasonable expectations of ourselves. We can try, fail, learn, and grow, harvesting hope rather than despair from our unsuccessful ventures.

THE REDEEMABLE FALL

God's grace in the midst of failure is clearly demonstrated in the life of Joseph, Jacob's favorite son. His experiences of failure and disappointment come primarily because of the machinations of those around him—he is the victim of others' jealousy.

Sold into slavery by his brothers, taken to Egypt, imprisoned unjustly, Joseph could have considered his life a failure and plunged into self-pity. But he remained faithful to God and to himself, even though he did not understand why these things were happening to him.

When his loyalty and wisdom resulted in his being promoted to second place in the kingdom, he was in a position to exercise vengeance against his brothers. But Joseph chose a different course. Instead of taking the opportunity to get revenge, he sought out God's purposes in his experiences of failure. "You intended to harm me," he told his brothers when they were reunited, "but God intended it for good" (Genesis 50:20).

Joseph was neither destroyed by his seeming failures nor angry at the injustices done to him. Long before he was reconciled with his brothers, he named his second son Ephraim, which means "twice fruitful." "God has made me fruitful in the land of my suffering," Joseph concluded (Genesis 41:52). As Joseph discovered, God can turn the worst of circumstances, the most abject of failures, into an opportunity for His glory to be displayed.

Nothing lies outside the reach of God's grace. Even Adam and Eve's deception and their ultimate fall into original sin are redeemed by God for His glory. Because mankind fell into sin, Christ came in the flesh to die for that sin. And because of His death and resurrection, men and women can be exalted to a higher level of fellowship with God—no longer merely creatures of the Creator, but sons and daughters of the Almighty, brothers and sisters of Jesus Christ Himself. Thus the Fall, though not God's original intention, was "redeemable." God not only restores what the evil destroyed, but turns the evil into greater good and the curse to greater blessing.

Some people—both Christian and nonChristian—have distorted this concept, saying that sin is therefore not sin because God can redeem it and bring good out of it. Paul, however, attacks such faulty reasoning:

> But where sin increased, grace increased all the more, so that, just as sin reigned in death, so also grace might reign through righteousness to bring eternal life through Jesus Christ our Lord.
> What shall we say, then? Shall we go on sinning so that grace may increase? By no means!
> (Romans 5:20-6:2)

God's ability and willingness to take the hardest struggles and most difficult life situations and turn them into blessing in no way negates the individual's responsibility for sin. When we choose wrongly, as did Adam and Eve— and as every human being since the Fall has—we are held responsible before God for our sin. We must repent, turn away from sin, and make restitution to those we have wronged. Often, even after we have been forgiven, we must live with the results of our sinful choices. But as God's grace intervenes in our lives, He can turn the curse into a blessing.

Thus our individual failures can also be redeemable falls. Because God's grace always reaches down to lift us up, restore us, and heal us, our failures can become a springboard to a life of deeper fellowship with Him, of greater understanding of ourselves, of gentler dealings with those around us. We have a High Priest who is able to sympathize with our weaknesses (Hebrews 4:15) and support us when we fall. He can turn our evil into good, our curse into a blessing, our failure into the ultimate success of becoming like Christ. God, through His grace, can make us fruitful in the land of our suffering.

FAILURE IS GOOD FOR THE SOUL

In the economy of God's grace, nothing—not even failure— is wasted. God can use the worst, the toughest, the most heart-wrenching experiences we endure to draw us closer to Himself and teach us the principles of living like Jesus. We need not fold up and withdraw when we fail; nor do we have to defend ourselves and try to appear perfect. And we do not have to mistake circumstance for character and name ourselves "failures." We can, instead, face our responsibilities squarely, learn from our mistakes, and grow.

Although it was difficult for me to believe when Dr. Bolen gave me my first F, failure was, indeed, good for my soul. My professor's firm but loving reprimand taught me an important lesson in grace: Failure can be the turning point that draws me into a deeper understanding of God's ability to bring good out of evil.

CHAPTER FOUR

Balancing Priorities

Drop thy still dews of quietness
Till all our strivings cease,
Take from our souls the strain
and stress
And let our ordered lives confess
The beauty of thy peace.
JOHN GREENLEAF WHITTIER

Randy never entered a room normally, and today was no exception. He flung open the restaurant door, rushed down the aisle, skidded to a stop beside the booth, and collapsed breathlessly across the table from me.

"Sorry I'm late," he gasped. "I just got caught up in some other things, and . . . ."

I smiled. Randy's story was always the same. He searched his pockets until he found a battered appointment calendar. "See?" he demanded, waving the smudged pages under my nose for verification. "I always overcommit myself; I've just got to get my priorities in order."

Randy's conclusion that he needed to get his priorities

in order is a common one—and not without a grain of truth. Certainly Randy's priorities (or lack of them) affected the chaotic jumble he called a schedule. But like many of us, Randy confused his goals and deadlines with priorities. He did not realize that what we do is only symptomatic, the outward evidence of our inward state. The important issue in establishing priorities is not so much *what we do*, but *who we are*.

We want to serve God, to grow, to be a positive influence in the lives of others, to be successful, respected, and admired; we want to glorify God with our lives. But often we get the cart first and the horse second. We get so caught up in "glorifying God" that we neglect, as the Westminster Confession teaches, to "enjoy Him."

Establishing priorities is a heart issue based on our motivations—the "why" behind what we do. Goals are our active, tangible response to those established priorities. So until our priorities are clear, the practical business of doing what God calls us to do will likely be a confusing and disorderly process.

CLARIFYING PRIORITIES

If you ask most Christians what vision they have for ongoing spiritual growth in their lives, what priorities they live by, you are apt to get a variety of "should" responses: "I should spend more time in Bible study," or "I should be more consistent in my prayer life." We tend to set goals according to what we think our priorities *should be*, according to what we have been taught, according to the expectations of the Christian community that surrounds us.

But the same well-meaning Christians who load themselves with shoulds end up burned out and broken down, with fragmented families and frazzled nerves. Something is wrong when we exhaust ourselves in the service of the Lord. We need reason; we need balance.

ME FIRST: PRIDE

You'd think Rob was a nice guy when you first met him. Jovial, always full of fun, Rob seemed inevitably to be the center of attention. He was a good plumber and a hard worker, too—or so he'd tell you. But when Rob was responsible for doing a job for the church, he'd grumble and complain, waste time, and generally produce a slipshod effort. When confronted, Rob's response was predictable: "The job's done, isn't it? It's good enough."

The chip on Rob's shoulder was most evident when he was home. There the universe revolved around him, or else it stopped altogether. Everyone bowed to Rob's schedule, and rearranged their lives to accommodate his desires. Rob accepted their service as if it were his due, with never a word of appreciation. He could never accept correction, admit fault, or even entertain the suggestion that he might not be right, yet he claimed to be living in service to the Lord.

Pride is a subtle, insidious enemy to godliness, wisely identified as first among the seven deadly sins (Proverbs 6:16-19). When we are first in our own hearts, the result is clear in our lives—if not to us, then to those around us. Rob's pride and self-centeredness hindered his relationships both with the Lord and with those around him. By putting himself first, he lost one of the greatest joys of the Christian life—the experience of grace in loving and serving others.

OTHERS FIRST: MARTYRDOM

Elizabeth was an ideal wife, an ideal mother, an ideal servant of the church. She gave everything for everyone. She worked hard to please her husband; she was at the beck and call of her two teenage children; she hosted slumber parties for her daughter and hockey parties for her son; she took meals to the housebound, visited the sick, taught Sunday school, and volunteered two afternoons a week at the Sheltered Workshop.

Then one day, Elizabeth broke. Hospitalized and tranquilized, she watched bleakly as her children drifted away to their own pursuits and her husband grew increasingly distant. She couldn't even cry anymore, so she simply whispered, "What happened? I tried so hard, so hard. . . ."

Many of us, in varying degrees of intensity, share Elizabeth's experience. We try so hard. We want to make other people happy, and the church applauds our efforts. Our lives center around performance, around self-sacrifice. "J-O-Y," we sing. "Jesus first, others second, yourself last: that's the way to spell J-O-Y."

For much too long, the church has bought into the deception that "burning yourself out for Jesus" is somehow an honorable and noble thing to do. We are encouraged to sacrifice ourselves on the altar of service, to give ourselves fully to family, friends, and church, all in the name of Jesus.

What we fail to realize is that Elizabeth's martyrdom is every bit as self-centered as Rob's arrogance, only we have learned to praise Elizabeth and condemn Rob. Seventeenth-century Archbishop Francois Fenelon writes, "If we had the light to discern it, we should see clearly that when we think we are humbling ourselves we are exalting ourselves; when we think we are annihilating ourselves we are seeking our own life."[1]

Martyrdom, as much as self-centered pride, exalts us above the Lord. But there is only one sacrifice that is acceptable: the sacrificial death of Christ. All our self-generated sacrificial acts result only in a downward spiral of works-righteousness, a performance trap that can effect no permanent change in our hearts.

Such "modest pride," Fenelon concludes, is a subtle and dangerous form of self-exaltation. "It is hungry for the esteem of good people. It wants to love so that it will be loved, and so that others will be impressed by its unselfishness. It only seems to forget itself in order to make itself more interesting to everyone."[2]

CHRIST FIRST: ORDER

Fenelon's words hit all too close to home. In the almost twenty years since I came into a relationship with Christ, I *thought* that my actions were based on biblical priorities. I studied the Scriptures, prayed regularly, pursued obedience, led others to the Lord, taught the Word, and discipled leaders who now minister throughout the world.

But recently, as the Lord worked to change some lifelong patterns of sin in my life, I came to a startling revelation about myself. Although I had *said* that my highest priority was God, my *real* priority had been maintaining an image of myself as a Christian leader. What people thought about me had become more important than what my life really was before God. The image had to be maintained at any cost; the drive to protect myself led to deception and duplicity.

The problem is, of course, that we do not know our own hearts, our secret motivations. The heart is deceitful and desperately wicked; only God knows it fully, and only He can reveal its truths to us (see Jeremiah 17:9-10). Even when we gain insight into the truth about ourselves, we cannot change ourselves. Only God can work lasting change in our lives. Only He can establish the inner priorities of the heart that will please Him.

God has showed us in His Word what His priorities are

and what is important to Him. He has established a *universal priority* around which all creation centers:

> He [Jesus] is the image of the invisible God, the first-born over all creation. For by him all things were created: . . . all things were created by him and for him. He is before all things, and in him all things hold together. And he is the head of the body, the church; he is . . . the firstborn from among the dead, so that *in everything he might have the supremacy.* For God was pleased to have all his fullness dwell in him, and through him to reconcile to himself all things.
> (Colossians 1:15-20, emphasis added)

God has set His Son at the center of the universe "that He [Christ] Himself might come to have first place in everything" (verse 18, NASB).

This universal priority that God has instituted is intended also to be the crucial *personal priority* by which God's people live. When Jesus Christ has "first place" in everything in our lives, when He comes "before all things," then our lives "hold together" in Him. He brings order out of chaos, and productivity out of commotion.

As much as we'd like to think so, centering our lives on Jesus and redeeming our personal priorities does not happen instantly and automatically when we become Christians. Our priorities, like most other things in this fallen, bent world, need the touch of God to bring them back into order.

THE JUGGLING ACT

Today is January 2. Since December 23, I have had overnight guests in my home for nine consecutive days. The holiday season included two deaths, one in-town funeral, one relative hospitalized, and thirty-four people for lunch.

Every year between Christmas and New Year's Day, I make plans for the coming year—not resolutions, exactly, but goals and long-range dreams. This year I recorded in my journal such lofty intentions as reading a book a month, not working weekends, making myself take more leisure time, and spending time in the afternoons in worship and meditation. Today, already behind in my work schedule, I reviewed those goals and thought, "Who am I kidding? On paper my life looks balanced; in reality, it's a juggling act."

Most of us, I suppose, struggle with the juggling-act mentality when we seek to establish priorities. Like Randy, we carry around our battered appointment calendars, and if we manage to fit in all the necessities, we think the day has been a success. We try desperately to keep all our oranges in the air; maybe we do all right with three or four, but when the guy offstage keeps throwing them at us, or when the oranges are replaced by sharpened sabers and flaming torches, we panic. The bills pile up and the pressure mounts; responsibilities within us and demands from without pull us in opposite directions; we lose control; we feel powerless; we say, "I've got to get my priorities in order."

QUIET BALANCE

For many Christians, the question, "How do I establish godly priorities?" is really, "How do I find balance in my life?" Most of us tend to be unbalanced: we work too much, or not enough. We give all to our loved ones, or we give nothing. We smother our children, or we ignore them. We burn out in service, or we occupy a pew.

I am a *doer*, a *planner*, a *worker*, a *fixer*. I can't chew gum because I go at it so intensely that I tire out my jaws. I've never learned to be moderate in any activity except housekeeping; whatever I do, I do at full speed, with full concentration—and, ultimately, with full exhaustion. I need the balance that God's grace can bring to my life, my plans, my priorities.

The primary issue of balance, certainly, is the recognition that *who I am is more important than what I do*. My value as a person is not dependent upon what I produce— whether it is evangelism decisions, sales increases, or well-disciplined children. My value to God—and ultimately to those I love—is based on *who I am in Jesus Christ.* I am, Ephesians 1:6 says, "accepted in the beloved" (KJV).

Just because God works from the inside out, of course, is no reason for me to be consigned to idleness, to spiritual thumb twiddling, waiting for the "miraculous transformation." My acceptance does not give me license to be lazy and sit around waiting for God to do something to me to make me mature or wise or exemplary.

Most of us have the opposite problem: We think we must work for and deserve God's love and interest in our lives. But we can never be good enough or do enough to earn God's loving intervention. Even if we could, He doesn't work that way. He offers grace freely, as a gift—not just for salvation, but continually, for every step in our walk with Christ. Once we realize that our value does not depend upon our own effort, we can be free from the demands of performance. We don't have to work harder, try harder, grit our teeth, and love harder. We can relax, quit juggling, and start balancing.

Focusing. If Jesus Christ is the central priority of the universe, it stands to reason that He should be the Christian's center, too. But focus means more than words about "looking to Jesus" and saying that Christ is on the throne of our heart.

Focus means accepting and responding to the charac ter of Christ *as the Bible presents Him*—which may some- times be quite different from the picture painted by the church. Jesus never promised, for example, that His follow- ers would live happy, trouble-free lives. In fact, He said just the opposite: "In this world you *will have trouble.* But take heart! I have overcome the world" (John 16:33, emphasis added).

A classic example of focusing upon the nature and grace of God appears in Brother Lawrence's *The Practice of the Presence of God.* A lay brother in a Carmelite monastery, Brother Lawrence was assigned to the kitchen crew. Yet even in the midst of the noise and chaos of his kitchen duties, he focused his inner spirit upon the Lord, conclud- ing that any duty done for the Lord's sake was holy service. No matter what his task, Brother Lawrence turned his heart toward God and found Him there in the midst of the most menial of labors.

Our struggles do not disappear when we focus on Christ, but they do come into perspective. As we worship, as we deepen in our knowledge of and relationship with the Lord, as we look to Him, He becomes the center and the foundation, the fulcrum upon which we balance *being* with *doing.*

Becoming. "Most people need to get more spiritually self- ish," a respected Bible teacher in my church once told me.

"Huh?" I responded. I had always been taught that selfishness was bad, a result of the Fall, a vice to be avoided. "I don't mean selfishness in a negative way," she explained. "Far too many people don't think enough of themselves. They ignore their own needs in trying to meet other people's desires, and they end up burning out. You can't give what you don't have."

Concentration upon our individual relationship with God is a key to becoming what God has created us to be. As we get in touch with our own strengths and weaknesses and catch a glimpse of the possibilities our life holds in God's hands, becoming that person takes on increased importance. We can give ourselves the time and the attention—physically, spiritually, and emotionally—to grow, to rest, to become whole people in Christ.

The priority of becoming involves others as well—family, friends, and loved ones. We become fully ourselves in relationship to others: As we commit time to deepen those relationships, we become richer, more loving, more compassionate people, better able to give of ourselves to meet others' needs.

Doing. What we do, certainly, is also important as we seek to establish our priorities: exercising spiritual disciplines, committing time and effort to our jobs, giving of ourselves in serving others, involving ourselves in church and community activities. But *doing* must grow out of *being;* external action must reflect internal character rather than acting as a substitute or a facade.

A young man grappling with his own place in God's plan and feeling desperately insignificant sought out his old mentor for advice and encouragement. For several hours they sat in silence on the shore of a small lake. The youth was beginning to be disappointed, for after his elaborate explanation of his problem, the mentor had said nothing. At last the old man picked up a stone, tossed it into the water, and pointed to the concentric circles spreading outward from the splash. "Behold the influence of a single life!" he said simply, then walked away.

The young man thought carefully about what his teacher had said. For a long time he had assumed that one person could do little to make a difference in the world. Then he realized that, whether he was aware of it or not, his life *did* influence others, like the stone thrown into the lake. Who he was and what he did had far-reaching consequences, circling out from himself to those around him— eventually, as one circle touched another, to those he did not even know. One life *does* make a difference. As we choose to focus our lives on Christ, we can have a profound effect for good on those around us.

"WHEREVER YOU ARE, BE THERE!"

Kathy was clearly frustrated with her friend Kelly. Kelly, for all her good intentions, was becoming increasingly scattered and disjointed. She couldn't remember appointments, was perpetually late, and often made her friends repeat what they had said because she wasn't paying close enough attention.

Finally, in a moment of exasperation, Kathy said, "Kelly, for Heaven's sake—wherever you are, *be there!*"

Kathy's advice to Kelly echoes the exhortation of Scripture: "Whatever your hand finds to do, do it with all your might" (Ecclesiastes 9:10).

Many of us struggle with learning to "be there" wherever we are. We half-listen to our children, thinking about problems at work. We give half-attention to our jobs, in turmoil over conflicts at home. We are distracted during worship by thoughts of the football game that starts at noon, and we choose the newspaper instead of a spouse's company over morning coffee.

Some things, of course, have to be done simply because they are part of the everyday movement of life:

doing the laundry, changing the oil in the car, shoveling the sidewalk, walking the dog. These activities may not demand or deserve our full commitment and our total attention. But as we consider the significant activities of our lives—relationships, worship, work, leisure—around the central priority of Christ, we can learn to focus our attention, to give full value to the moment at hand.

The world often perceives the "big things" as the important measure of a person's life—success, accomplishment, material gains, influence, power. For the Christian, the "little things" are important—our attitudes, our secret desires, the contentment of our hearts, the care we express toward other people and the world around us.

Attention to the "little things" is exemplified in the actions of a friend of mine. She used to go out on her daily walks with a plastic trash bag. As she walked, meditated, and prayed, she picked up bottles, cans, and hamburger wrappers from the much-used trail along the lake. She took the time and the effort to make this small stretch of the world more pleasant, not just for herself, but for those who came after her. She redeemed that walk by making it more beautiful, by restoring the area from the damage other people had left behind.

Few people ever knew of the effect of my friend's effort. No one thanked her for cleaning up or praised her for caring. But, like Brother Lawrence, she recognized the most menial of tasks as an act of worship, a participation in the redemption of God's world.

"The chief end of man," according to the Westminster Confession, "is to glorify God and enjoy Him forever." Such a priority is not a demand for works, but for focus. Christ, as first place in our lives, holds everything else together. By His grace, He allows us to attend to *becoming*, and *doing* follows.

CHAPTER FIVE

Redefining Maturity

The child is father of the man;
And I could wish my days to be
Bound each to each by natural piety.
WILLIAM WORDSWORTH

W hen I was little, my father had a unique philosophy about gardening—one that he maintains to this day. "If it's a bad year," he quipped, "nobody's gonna get anything anyway; if it's a good year, everybody will give you what you need."

On a good year, the vines overflowed with red, juicy tomatoes—sweet, rich fruit, ripened slowly in the hot summer sun. We ate them whole, like apples. On a bad year, we didn't bother with the tomatoes at all—the ones in the grocery store had a waxy, artificial look and a taste like plastic. They were hothouse tomatoes, grown indoors and picked green, ripening on the way to the wholesaler's.

Hothouse tomatoes were grown exclusively for their monetary value; we were certain that no thought whatsoever was given to their flavor. They were produced fast and efficiently, but the speed showed in the result.

The church today is full of hothouse tomatoes—people whose lives are marked by fast-forward maturity. Unwilling to take the time—or the heat—necessary for natural growth, we pump ourselves full of spiritual vitamins, load up with teaching, accumulate some head knowledge, and drop from the vine green. When the skin turns red, when we look as if we have it all together, we are declared "mature" and sent forth to plant the seeds of our unripe faith in someone else's garden.

The process of hothouse maturity is especially prevalent in the lives of Christian celebrities. When famous people make commitments to Christ, they are immediately exalted as authorities on the faith and examples to emulate. They may be struggling with their own faith and desperately in need of guidance and time to grow, but they are often thrust into the spotlight rather than nurtured and cared for. We expect—and demand—instant maturity.

But maturity—that elusive state of "having arrived"—is not a valid goal for the Christian. In one sense, of course, we can say that we mature as we grow deeper in faith and come to trust Christ more completely. But even Paul, whose teachings comprise more than half the New Testament, declared that he did not consider himself as having obtained that goal. "I press on," he says, "to take hold of that for which Christ Jesus took hold of me" (Philippians 3:12).

GOD'S TIMETABLE

Most of us, at one time or another, have longed to reach some magic "age of independence" when we would be mature, respected as adults. We find, of course, that adulthood is much overrated; as "grownups" we have a whole new set of problems and difficulties. Yet even spiritually, we often cling to the hope that one day we will wake up mature, able to handle all the problems that face us, perceived as spiritual giants—or at least spiritual adults—by those around us.

Just as physical growth takes many years and much struggle, spiritual maturity comes hard as well. It takes time to grow; time to learn and mature—and the process isn't as simple in reality as it looks on paper. When we strive against the time necessary for our development, we live in frustration. But when we can relax in God's timetable for our growth, depending upon His grace for the work His Spirit wants to do in our lives, we can experience the joy and wonder of growth, change, and fruitfulness.

When Roberta came into a relationship with Christ, she was aware that many changes needed to take place. She had destructive habit patterns that needed to be dealt with, broken relationships that needed to be mended, and a lifetime of self-dependence that needed to be remedied. But to Roberta's surprise, the changes that began to take place as the Lord worked in her life affected none of the "obvious" areas in which she needed growth. Instead of dealing with surface issues that were only symptoms of Roberta's deeper problems, the Lord went straight to the heart of the issue and pinpointed her rebellion.

A year or two into her Christian life, Roberta was doing all the "right" things—reading the Bible, praying, attending corporate worship, submitting herself to the accountability of a small group. Yet most of the areas that she felt needed changing in her life still seemed untouched. She had tried— oh, how she had tried—to break those bad habits, to change her attitudes, to wrestle maturity out of her performance.

But it didn't seem to be working well at all.

Her friends tried to help. They told her what to do and how to do it; they prayed for changes in her life; they gave her free advice about altering her behavior.

"I give up!" Roberta finally said in frustration. "I've done everything I know to do; I don't think I'll ever grow up! Well, if God wants me changed, He'll just have to do it; I can't do any more."

Roberta came to the end of her rope. Having done all, she gave up. And gradually, as His time was fulfilled in her life, the Lord worked the changes *she* wanted to see. But long before, God had already been working the changes that were important to *Him.*

THE GRACE OF GROWTH

In Colossians 2:6, Paul holds out an important key for Christian maturity: "Just as you received Christ Jesus as Lord, continue to live in him." We readily acknowledge that we receive Christ by grace through faith, as a gift of God, apart from any merit or deserving on our own part. But then, strangely, we seem somehow to move into a "performance mentality": We think that, once salvation is accomplished, we have to do the rest ourselves.

By perceiving "maturity" as an accomplishment we need to attain as quickly as possible, we miss the grace of God in the process of growth. If we intend to walk in Christ as we have received Him, we must understand that growing in Christ is a journey, not a destination. God is in control both of the timing and the development of our spiritual growth.

The Bible clearly tells us that Jesus is "the author and perfecter of our faith" (Hebrews 12:2), the One "who began a good work" in us and "will carry it on to completion"

(Philippians 1:6). Christ, through His gracious work in our lives, gives growth and brings us to spiritual stability. No matter how hard we try, we cannot accomplish that work ourselves. Not only do we lack the ability to make the spiritual changes necessary, but we often do not even *know* what changes are on God's agenda.

Too often in the Body of Christ we try to rush ourselves—or others—through to the "end product." We prize that ambiguous achievement called "maturity," and end up focusing on surface issues.

In his ode *Intimations of Immortality*, William Wordsworth describes the process by which society (including religious society) imposes its standards and values upon the coming generation. The child quickly discovers what pleases his elders and learns, by imitation, how to fulfill their expectations of him.

> The little actor cons another part;
> Filling from time to time his "humorous stage"
> With all the Persons, down to palsied Age
> That life brings with her in her equipage;
> As if his whole vocation
> Were endless imitation.[1]

Regrettably, the Christian community operates the same way. We surround people with a cultural standard of faith, and we make our expectations manifestly clear: having devotions every day; maintaining a consistent prayer life; speaking the jargon that makes us sound spiritually mature. And because we look at the appearance rather than at the heart to judge our maturity levels, we establish an elaborate system of Pharisaism in which our "righteousness" is founded on performance.

Our responsibility before God, however, is not to try to

do better, to make ourselves more pleasing to God, to grow ourselves up. Our responsibility is *obedience*, and obedience is quite different from *performance*. God does not demand that we *do* anything for Him or *accomplish* anything for our own spiritual growth. He only requires that we *submit* to Him and respond to the work of His Spirit in our lives.

REDEFINING MATURITY

"Sometimes I don't know if I'll ever grow up!" Diana exclaimed. At age forty-two, a successful business consultant with her own home and good prospects for the future, Diana had returned to her parents' home to spend the Christmas holidays. "Something strange happens when I go home," she confessed. "I turn into a teenager again. I argue with my mother over trivial matters; I'm just not myself. Will I ever be an adult when I'm with my parents?"

Diana's dilemma is a common one, spotlighting a troublesome problem about maturity: It doesn't happen all at the same time. Adolescents struggle with this truth: While they may have arrived at physical maturity, their corresponding emotional and mental development has not yet caught up with their bodies. As a result, they often have a hard time restraining the demands of an adult body when they still have the emotional resources of a child.

Similarly, adults who are otherwise controlled and mature, who have spiritual depth and emotional stability, may nevertheless have certain areas in their lives in which they are still children, unable to handle stress, or uncertain how to respond. These remnants of the child in each of us may produce a delightful childlike wonder about life or an irritating, demanding, childish response to difficulty—depending upon the circumstances and the person.

Recently a friend had a new one-piece corner shower installed in her home. It was beautiful—a sleek, flawless, shining example of modern technology in almond-colored enamel. But the first time it was used, a crack appeared in the corner. When the repairman came to fix it, he explained what happened. "Sometimes tiny air pockets develop between the enamel coating and the fiberglass backing. Everything looks fine, but the first time any pressure is applied to the shower—like the weight of someone stepping into it—the enamel coating cracks because it doesn't move with the more flexible fiberglass."

Like people, I thought. No matter how well we cope with the stresses of adult life, no matter how responsible we are, no matter how spiritually mature we seem to be, we are likely to have hidden pockets of immaturity under the surface, just waiting for outside pressure to break through the shining facade.

Often we respond to the revelation of the child within by telling ourselves or others, "Grow up!" But we are not equipped to act on that advice, any more than an infant can cook his own dinner or change his own diapers. Growth and change take place on God's schedule, not ours. Perhaps what we need is not a greater effort to force ourselves into a predetermined pattern for development, but a redefinition of maturity based, not on our own performance record, but on God's grace.

GROWING DEEPER

Spiritual growth is often compared to physical growth: birth, infancy, childhood, adolescence, adulthood. The Bible makes use of the parallel—being born again, craving spiritual milk, growing up to take in the meat of the Word, becoming spiritual mothers and fathers.

Although the image is basically a biblical one, it is so familiar that it is often overused and little understood. And it tempts us to see spiritual development as an upward movement, a ladder that we climb to get to the top, to draw closer to God and please Him more effectively.

The child, however, has no control over how fast he grows, how tall he gets, or how rapidly he matures. He faces certain choices that enable his development—lifestyle choices, obedience to authority, choice of friends, openness to spiritual influences, dedication to studies. He can make certain decisions that facilitate his maturity, but more often than not he is unaware of maturity as a motivation—it is a secondary result of his choices. He obeys his parents because he wants to avoid punishment; he studies because he is rewarded for good grades; he accepts responsibility because he desires the accompanying privileges.

Maturity, like happiness, is a byproduct of life, not a goal to be aimed for. We cannot make ourselves mature— nor can we push others into maturity. But as we submit to God and obey Him, as we learn and apply His Word, as we focus on developing Christlike attitudes and actions, we go deeper in our understanding of and relationship with the Lord who made us in His image. We grow to be more like Jesus Christ.

The old Victorian house I live in is surrounded by trees—some of them massive oaks, as old as the house itself, others more recently planted birches and maples. As spring comes, the younger trees bud first, bringing out their fresh green leaves as visible signs of life. But the hundred-year-old oaks are slower; their gnarled branches remain bare when everything else has turned green. Maturity is not always confirmed merely by the outward signs.

Perhaps real spiritual maturity could be defined in terms of deepening, growing into a close, intimate relationship with God—and ultimately with others. A tree with shallow roots may look good from the outside, but it does not have the stability to withstand the storms and winds that come. When our roots go down deep into the bedrock of faith, we not only produce good fruit, but we have the strength to endure times of drought and stormy weather.

WHO'S WHO IN SPIRITUAL GROWTH?

I grew up among educators. My mother was a secondary teacher; I became a college professor; many of my friends have careers in education. Educators all say the same thing: "You learn more from your students than you'll ever teach."

That statement always fascinated and puzzled me—until I was thrust into teaching. Then I began to wonder, "Who's who here? Who is the teacher, and who is the student?" And I learned, over the years, that the division between *instructor* and *instructee* is a fine line indeed.

We are all students. We are all teachers. We are all workers together for the building up of Christ's Body. Each of us has something to offer, something to learn. And we defeat the purpose of fellowship when we perceive spiritual growth as a group of truths imparted from the haves to the have-nots.

PLAYING WITHOUT SCORECARDS

Once I attended a conference designed to meet the needs of writers at many different levels of experience. The meeting was crowded with beginners—would-be writers who had never published at all. Yet when the workshop hour began, the workshop entitled "Basic Writing" had to be canceled. Nobody showed up; nobody wanted to be classified as a "beginner."

In the Christian church, similarly, people often resist being known as a new Christian or a baby believer—and understandably so. The "stages of growth" image we use for Christian maturity is often perceived as a hierarchy of right-eousness: the "more mature" you get, the higher up the scale you go, the more you're respected, admired, and heeded.

But growth in Christ is not so easily categorized. Just as we all have "air pockets" of immaturity hidden beneath the surface, so we all have gifts, abilities, and wisdom to share with those around us. If we want to grow in God's grace and extend that grace to others, we need to quit keeping score, abandon our external measures of maturity, and focus on the root systems of our relationship with Jesus Christ.

GROWING UP, GROWING CLOSE

In recent years much attention has been given to the so-called "Peter Pan/Cinderella Syndrome": people who refuse to grow up, take responsibility for themselves, and leave their selfish childishness behind them. Most of us know both men and women who, although mature in the physical sense, are far from mature emotionally.

In spiritual terms, too, real grownup-ness involves much more than simply plodding through a measured number of years. Age does not necessarily bring wisdom, nor does youth imply immaturity. Spiritual depth, like emo-tional maturity, comes through experience and is marked by responsibility, direction, and intimacy.

Spiritually mature people take responsibility for themselves. Since that fateful day when Adam said, "The woman made me do it," humans have made excuses for themselves, blamed others, and searched for a scapegoat for their wrongdoings. Spiritual development, however, is marked by responsibility, such as David demonstrated when he owned up to his sin with Bathsheba. David's sin was clearly wrong, but the manner in which he dealt with it is a principle we would do well to emulate.

Spiritual adults not only take responsibility for admitting their faults and making things right, they also accept the accountability for their own spiritual growth and for helping others find their way.

I once heard a pastor say, "You are as spiritually mature as you want to be. If you're not as close to the Lord as you'd like, don't blame the pastor, or your parents, or your children, or your church, or your busy schedule. Your spiritual development is your responsibility, and you are accountable to the Lord for yourself." He did not mean, of course, that we automatically become mature simply by expressing the desire, but that we can make choices that facilitate the deepening of our relationship with the Lord. Maturity is the work of God's grace; we can cooperate with that work by focusing on the Spirit's purposes in our lives and allowing Him to change us, to conform us more fully to the image of Christ.

Spiritually mature people have a sense of direction. Direction does not always mean that we know precisely where we're going; it does mean that we know where we've been, who we are, and to whom we look for our focus and guidance. Jesus Himself demonstrated that direction as He prepared for His coming death: "Jesus knew that the Father had put all things under his power, and that he had come from God and was returning to God; so he . . . began to wash his disciples' feet" (John 13:3-5).

As we mature in Christ, we gain a sense of security in our identity in the Lord. We don't have to prove ourselves or play one-upmanship games with others in the Body of Christ. We can serve others as Jesus did, because our focus is on God rather than on our own reputation. And whether His direction leads to fame and success or to anonymous service, we can rest in His control, knowing who we belong to, that we have come from God and will return to God.

Spiritually mature people pursue intimacy. The Peter-Pan person, the individual who doesn't want to grow up, usually is incapable of real intimacy, because intimacy is based on selflessness. Developing intimate relationships with God and others requires a measure of selflessness, of putting others' concerns and needs before our own.

As fallen human beings, our motives are probably never completely pure; there is always an underlying, often unconscious, self-centeredness at work in our lives. But the mature person is aware of that core of selfishness and tries to reach beyond it, to give himself freely to God in worship and to others in love and friendship.

Intimacy implies reality: stepping out from behind our facades, allowing ourselves to be seen and known, and accepting others for who they are as well. In the physical process of growing up, maturing is a long-term movement toward independence, a gradual weaning away from parents. But spiritual growth brings us to greater reliance upon our heavenly Father, a closer relationship, a deeper level of dependence. Spiritual maturity brings an intimacy with God. We learn to know Him, to respond to His Word and understand some of His purposes in our lives. We live in dependence upon His grace and in the realization that He operates in our lives for our good. We learn to love Him—not merely to say the right words, but to sense His presence with us. And intimacy with God frees us for intimacy with others.

RECEIVING THE GRACE OF GROWTH

When we learn to perceive spiritual growth as a gift of God's grace rather than an achievement accomplished by personal effort, we allow ourselves—and others—the freedom to fail, to be afraid, to be childlike. Because the maturing of each life may take a far different course than anyone else's growth, we don't have to compare ourselves with the apparent progress of any other Christian. We no longer have to be embarrassed to say, "I don't know," or afraid to ask questions. Under grace, we can simply relax and live, modeling for those around us the liberty of grace—our emancipation from pretense.

Freedom in the Spirit, certainly, differs from what the world calls "freedom." Under grace, we are not at liberty to excuse sin or to persist in selfishness because we "haven't reached that point in maturity." Relaxing under grace does not give us the license to go our own way, but the freedom and the ability to go *God's* way.

Spiritual maturity is not a ladder that we climb or a goal that we aim for. It is, rather, the process of becoming all God has called us to be as individuals. We don't have to compete for the "Mature Christian of the Year" award; we don't have to be hothouse tomatoes rushed to market on an arbitrary time schedule. We can, instead, ripen naturally on the vine, producing sweet fruit and good seed.

CHAPTER SIX

Will the Real Me Please Stand Up!

*The man who has no inner life
is the slave to his surroundings.*
HENRI FREDERIC AMIEL

Frustrated and depressed, I arrived at the sorority house to meet with Sheila. After her conversion, I had helped Sheila grow in her Christian life. We had been sharing together for several months. But I didn't feel much like a disciplemaker at the moment; pressed in with a variety of stresses and struggles, I simply wanted to go away and cry for a while. I sat down and poured out my problems to her.

"Get real!" Sheila responded. "You? You're always on top of things; I never thought you had those kinds of struggles."

GET REAL

The phrase still haunts me. For twenty years I have sought to walk with the Lord, to be honest with others, to let them see the truth of my life. I failed. I wanted people to approve of me, respect me, applaud me, and so I covered up. I let others see surface struggles, the insignificant pain I endured. But I hid my real self, my deepest secrets, my most devastating sins, the emotional struggles I battled most of my life.

Being authentic is easier said than done. We all tend to put up fronts. T. S. Eliot's title character in "The Love Song of J. Alfred Prufrock" speaks of preparing "a face to meet the faces that you meet."[1] Consciously or subconsciously, we want people to look up to us and to perceive us as strong, capable, trusting Christians, well on the road to perfection. We may even convince ourselves, as I did, that others expect perfection of us, that we will lose respect and authority in ministry if we allow others to see our struggles and failures.

Sometimes, in fact, people do turn away from us when we allow them to see who we really are. Some Christians may be unable to forgive our sin, even when God has forgiven and restored us. And some people never forget once they have been disappointed. In the short run, we appear to lose by being honest about our struggles.

But covering up can be even more devastating—both for ourselves and for others. Often those who are themselves struggling to find a foothold for their faith are repelled rather than attracted by the facade of perfection. After all, they reason, how can someone who has it all together understand and sympathize with my pitiful attempts to get my head above water? Won't someone who has lived through the struggle be better equipped to help me cope and find a measure of victory?

We have all, of course, "lived through the struggle"; all

of us experience pain, heartbreak, doubt, frustration, anger. But when we hesitate to let other people see our vulnerable* places, we present an image far different from the reality of our own inner chaos. And that facade—that wall—divides us both from those we might be able to help and from the support we ourselves so desperately need.

WHO AM I, ANYWAY?

During the turbulent '60s, many of us set out to "find ourselves." We roamed the streets of San Francisco or New Orleans in jeans and floppy hats, flowers in our hair and guitars slung across our backs. We picketed for civil rights and against the Vietnam War. But many of us, years after the tear gas cleared, were still asking: Who am I, anyway?

It's not an insignificant question. Most of us answer not by telling *who we are*, but by telling *what we do*. Who am I? I'm a teacher, a dentist, a carpenter, a writer, a mother, a student, a farmer. We identify ourselves by our *performance* rather than by our *personhood*.

The grace of God seeks to set us free from the pervasive performance mentality that has infused Christendom. My value in Christ is not dependent upon what I have done that is good, right, noble, or imitable. These efforts, the Bible tells me, are "filthy rags," worthless in God's sight to earn me His favor and love (Isaiah 64:6). Only Christ Himself has done what needed to be done; the rest is grace, freely given—if I can only accept it. My value and worth as a person rest in who Christ is and who I am as God's child.

Discovering who I am is not simply a matter of submitting myself to the lordship of Jesus Christ. If it were that easy, Christianity would be a very attractive faith, full of well-adjusted, emotionally healthy people. The gospel of prosperity fails us when we seek easy answers for difficult questions. Whitewashing the tomb does not resurrect the bones within. Many Christians endure lifelong struggles with self-image and deep emotional agony as they grapple with real, internal problems that cannot be solved by superficial solutions.

There are no easy answers; there are not even any easy questions. Years of conditioning reinforce the compulsion to earn our self-worth through performance. But by God's grace, we can stop focusing on ourselves—our own image— and look to Him, who gives us our value.

WHY DON'T I LIKE "ME" MUCH?

The great evangelist Charles H. Spurgeon inspired many young preachers, men who traveled with him and learned from him. It is reported that one of these young men noticed the odd assortment of people who came to hear the famous man preach. Pulling Spurgeon aside, the young minister asked his mentor, "Mr. Spurgeon, why are there so many strange people who come to your meetings?"

"It's simple," Spurgeon reputedly answered. "Light attracts bugs."

The same can be said about the Church. Light attracts bugs—and some of the strangest are those we face in the mirror each morning. God Himself said He had chosen a "peculiar people" (Deuteronomy 26:18, KJV)—and the modern definition of "peculiar" fits quite well.

Unfortunately, we have difficulty coming to grips with our peculiarity. Most of us don't like ourselves very much; we're too fat or too thin, too outgoing or too shy. We put our foot in our mouth with alarming regularity. We always seem to do what irritates our loved ones, and we can't make anything come out right. Intellectually we believe that God doesn't make mistakes, but emotionally we're pretty sure that we're the exception to that rule. We have a hard time living at peace with ourselves.

In many of his letters, the Apostle Paul greets the believers with the salutation, "Grace and peace to you from God our Father and from the Lord Jesus Christ" (Romans 1:7)—a greeting that is incorporated into many liturgical worship services today. As Paul presents the good news to the believers in Rome, he summarizes the connection between grace and peace:

> Therefore, since we have been justified through faith, we have peace with God through our Lord Jesus Christ, through whom we have gained access by faith into this grace in which we now stand. (Romans 5:1-2)

Peace with God can never be achieved through our own deeds, our own merit, our own works. We are buggy, peculiar people, and we often don't measure up to our own standards. Only through faith by grace, as we rest in the security of Jesus' love for us, can we have peace with God— and, subsequently, with ourselves.

In practical terms, entering into peace with God means acknowledging that I am not worthy of all He has done for me. I am a sinner, deserving only condemnation. I can never come to peace with God through my own effort or performance; no matter how much I do, my sinful condition still plagues me. I can try and try, and never be good enough to measure up. And yet, with a depth of love I cannot comprehend, He accepts me, welcomes me, values me.

I may never experience the kind of love and commitment I deeply desire on a human level; I may never know the joy of a mutual relationship with someone I cherish. But I can know, at least in part, the unconditional love and acceptance that God offers me.

One of the profound truths of living in God's grace is that we don't have to "have it all together." We don't have to know the answers, to be wise and mature, to live on a plane above the rest of humanity. We live as human beings— fallen people, aware of our shortcomings, and making the best of what we've got. The Serenity Prayer, composed by Dr. Reinhold Niebuhr in 1943, offers valuable insight into self-acceptance:

> God, give us grace to accept with serenity the things that cannot be changed, courage to change the things that should be changed, and the wisdom to distinguish the one from the other.

AUTHENTIC CHRISTIANITY

The Bible study discussion always came to a screeching halt when Elizabeth began to speak. Her accounts of suffering, persecution, and discipline threw a pall over the atmosphere of the group.

"Elizabeth," one member asked, "doesn't anything *good* ever happen in your life?"

"I'm just being real," Elizabeth countered. "Life isn't all roses, you know."

"But with Jesus in your life," Sarah piped up, "you are able to live victoriously above your problems!" She went on with a five-minute catalog of victories, ending triumphantly with, "Since I met Jesus, life has just been so wonderful!"

Many of us have discovered some Elizabeths and some Sarahs in the fellowships we frequent. Either of these two extremes can be mistaken for transparency in the Christian faith. But real faith neither focuses upon the negative nor hides behind positive thinking. Nor is it, as some interpret, "spiritual exhibitionism," or "letting it all hang out." Not every aspect of our relationship with the Lord and with others should be displayed to public view; not every problem should be flaunted, not every sin incorporated into public confession—especially when others would be hurt by such confession.

Transparency is not parading the past, playing "Who's Got the Spiciest Testimony?" with others in the Body of Christ. Being transparent does not mean living in a glass house; it means allowing others to see that our character matches up with the truths we profess, admitting our areas of struggle and turmoil. True transparency, the kind of authenticity that is glorifying to God and helpful to those around us, is balanced with wisdom and discretion.

REALITY

"For most of my life I've been controlled by the need to please other people," Laura confessed. "I did what others wanted, submitted to their tastes—first my parents and friends, later my husband and children. When my marriage broke up, I panicked. I was free to do what I wanted, but I didn't know what that was. I couldn't even pick out curtains for my apartment!"

Laura had exerted so much energy in pleasing others and conforming to their desires that she had lost touch with herself and with her own needs and feelings. She had difficulty being real, because she didn't know what her inner reality was.

Laura's case may be extreme, but many of us to one extent or another exert energy to maintain a facade that is different from reality. We fear that we may not be loved or accepted if the truth about us is known, and so we put up a front, trying to please others and trying to make ourselves seem more together than we are.

The Bible, however, calls us to be people of *integrity*. The term is derived from the root *integer*, meaning *one*; from that root springs the word *integrate*, to unify, to make complete.

If we are people of integrity, our outward behavior, attitudes, and methods of relating to others reflect what is in our hearts. We do not waste time and energy in an effort to make ourselves look good or to maintain a false image; rather, we focus on the Lord and His purposes and set our hearts toward obedience.

Jesus devoted a number of parables and images to the principle of reality: "You are the salt. . . . You are the light. . . . Let your light shine before men. . . . Every good tree bears good fruit" (Matthew 5:13-16, 7:17). We are called to let people see who we are and to share ourselves with those in need. But we are *never* called to pretend to be something we're not.

When we experience difficult times, we may be tempted to pretend that we are okay, and try to make our lives look good from the outside. Isaiah 50 offers both a consolation and a warning to us during those dark nights of the soul:

> Let him who walks in the dark,
> > who has no light,
> trust in the name of the LORD,
> > and rely on his God.
> But now, all you who light fires
> > and provide yourselves with flaming torches. . . .
> You will lie down in torment. (Isaiah 50:10-11)

When we walk in the dark, we do not have to pretend that we understand or that we can see. We can simply trust in

God's character and commit ourselves to Him. The torment comes when we light our own fires and attempt to find our way out of the struggle on our own. Not only do we frustrate ourselves, but we establish a pattern of deception, a facade that must be maintained.

Sad to say, we know the jargon far too well. We can speak the words of spiritual health and fool most of the people most of the time, while we die within. When we come into the darkness, we often are not content with honest dependence upon the God who is as close at midnight as He is at noon. Instead, we kindle our own fires, and we live in the torment of our own duplicity.

Freedom from that torment comes with integrity. When what is visible on the outside reflects the true condition of the inner person, we experience the liberty of integrity. As our hearts are turned toward God, others see the evidence of that commitment—not that we are free from sin and struggle, but that we depend upon the Lord for light, willing to sit in darkness if God's purposes are best accomplished there.

HONESTY

Living a life of integrity, in which the outward image truly reflects the inner character, gives us the freedom to be open with one another about our struggles, frustrations, and shortcomings. Paul called himself "chief of sinners" (1 Timothy 1:15, KJV) as well as "an apostle . . . set apart for the gospel of God" (Romans 1:1).

David was a man of integrity, a "man after [God's] own heart" (Acts 13:22). In the midst of a searing awareness of his own sinfulness, he was open and honest with God and others. David sinned greatly, sending Uriah to his death and marrying Bathsheba. But when confronted by the prophet

Nathan, David acknowledged his guilt: "I have sinned against the Lord" (2 Samuel 12:13).

Throughout the psalms, David offered a pattern for honesty and openness. He never denied the seriousness of his circumstances—whether attacks from without or sin festering within. In Psalm 27, for example, he gives a detailed, realistic account of his troubles: "Evil men advance against me to devour my flesh . . . my enemies and my foes attack me. . . . Do not hide your face from me. . . . Do not reject me or forsake me, O God my Savior" (verses 2,9). Then, in the midst of such realism, David inevitably turns again to focus on the Lord:

> I am still confident of this:
> > I will see the goodness of the LORD
> > in the land of the living.
> Wait for the LORD;
> > be strong and take heart
> > and wait for the LORD. (verses 13-14)

Real openness, in biblical terms, means first coming to a point of honesty with God. Often we tell ourselves—and each other—that we should respond "in faith" to whatever circumstances confront us, that we should simply trust God's control and be at peace.

Theoretically, such advice sounds good. But it's not always that easy. David's honesty with God includes anger, confusion, and frustration. We, too, as we experience both difficulty and joy, can bring our unexpurgated emotions before the Lord. He is, after all, big enough to withstand our anger (as long as we're not addressing it toward Him), wise enough to sort out our confusion, and patient enough to endure our frustration. Honesty with God does not necessarily undermine our reverence toward Him.

Only as we begin to be sincerely open with God can we relax enough to let our guard down and allow others to see both our struggles and our victories. We can laugh at ourselves when we fall over our own feet, use failure as a tool for growth, and discover the freedom to say, "I don't know."

DISCRETION

As we sat around the dinner table that Sunday afternoon, the conversation turned to Dennis and Diane, a couple in our church who had recently announced that they were expecting their second child. My host's young daughters listened intently, thrilled at the prospect of "the new baby."

Finally their youngest, age four, simply could wait no longer to offer her contribution to the conversation. She turned her round little cherub-face to me and said, confidentially, but in a voice loud enough to be heard by everyone at the table, "Well, you know, Mom's not going to have any more babies, 'cause the doctor fixed her just like he did the cat!"

After a long, meaningful pause, the child's father said in a low, controlled voice, "Rachel, sweetheart, you don't have to tell everything you know."

What to tell. In our eagerness to be open and honest with those around us, we often say too much too quickly, go too deep too fast. We need to be reminded that "we don't have to tell everything we know." We need to balance honesty with discretion.

Long before I became a Christian, and subsequently after my initial forays into the deep waters of faith, I struggled with the problem of telling too much. Plagued by the mistaken notion that honesty demanded exhibitionism, I habitually turned my friendships into a dumping ground for the garbage of the past and the gory details of the present.

One night in particular, I sought to share with the evening worship group at church certain problems I was encountering in a particular relationship. I *said* I wanted prayer; what I really wanted was sympathy. I poured out my frustration and bitterness for all to see, and my friend, who was present that night, left the meeting feeling violated and manipulated. It was many months before the friendship began to be reconciled, and then only as we worked and prayed through the problems together, without making public issue of them.

For others like me, who are naturally outgoing and open, the wisdom of knowing what not to tell often comes only through failure and heartbreak. Such discretion is not born out of self-protection, the hard shell of defense that cries, "I'll never be hurt again!" It is, rather, sensitivity to issues that might bring pain to others, and the peaceful acceptance that I don't have to tell everything I know.

Whom to tell. "I'm afraid to be honest with people," Keith confessed. "I'm a pastor, a spiritual leader. People don't always want to know the truth about the humanity of their leaders. And the church is notorious for shooting its wounded!"

Stunned by Keith's honesty, I nevertheless had to agree. It is possible to be too open, to make ourselves too vulnerable—or vulnerable in the wrong way—to people around us.

Being selective about sharing the deep problems and struggles in our lives in no way contradicts transparency. "Above all else, guard your heart," Proverbs 4:23 instructs. Irreparable damage can be done, both to the heart and to the testimony, by failing to guard our hearts, by sharing unwisely with those who can neither understand nor respect our candor.

To maintain that balance—not to fear openness, but to be wise in our vulnerability and discreet in our sharing—we need to remember that true transparency means allowing people to see not our *secrets* but our *character*—the character of Christ being formed in us. Our friends and acquaintances, Christian and nonChristian alike, need to see both our humanness and the touch of the Divine in our daily experiences.

TILL WE HAVE FACES

In C. S. Lewis's mythic novel *Till We Have Faces*, the central character, Princess Orual, offers a striking image of authenticity. Angry with the gods, Orual veils her face, and for many years never lets her countenance be seen. Finally, near the end of her life, having come to a reconciliation of her anger, she writes, "How can they [the gods] meet us face to face till we have faces?"[2]

We may be afraid for others to see us—or even to see ourselves—if we are depending upon our own self-created images or our own self-styled righteousness. Apart from the grace of God, we readily hide behind veils of unreality, whitewashing the tomb, creating a face to meet the faces that we meet. Only as we recognize and embrace the grace of God can we be set free from the bondage of such images, facing ourselves and each other.

CHAPTER SEVEN

The Grace to Be Misunderstood

*My conscience is captive to the Word
of God. . . . Here I stand;
I can do no other.*
MARTIN LUTHER

Many years ago, a handful of young Christians, searching for meaningful fellowship and training in ministry, developed a tight-knit group—a collection of believers dedicated, it seemed, to knowing and doing God's will. The group held great influence over its members, down to the tiniest detail of hairstyles, clothing styles, and lifestyles.

The group operated peacefully until one member began to make some unpopular choices about God's will and directions for her life. The group advocated dedication to home, marriage, and family as the only alternative for a woman's life; this individual felt called to a career. The group discouraged outside involvement except for purposes of evangelism; this person insisted upon maintaining previous friendships with nonbelievers. The group strongly favored a communal life; this young woman resisted being isolated from the rest of the world.

At last the final showdown came: "You're either for us or against us," the leader said. "Choose." With great sadness and a measure of fear, the young woman chose to leave the fellowship that had been the sole source of her spiritual nurturing for almost a year. And from that day on, none of the members of the group would acknowledge her or accept her overtures of friendship. She was cut off, isolated from the people she had loved and the fellowship she had known.

I was that woman. For years I tried in vain to explain myself, to make my motives understood by the people I had been so close to. I wanted them to believe that I was not a heretic or a reprobate. I desperately wanted to follow the leading of the Lord in my life; but His leading didn't seem to be their leading. I had to follow the direction I saw for myself, but that direction led me away from acceptance and into misunderstanding.

For many Christians, the desire to be understood and accepted is an issue of paramount importance. We all want others to approve of us, to understand our motives, to agree with what we do and why we do it. The drive to conform is a strong one, often conflicting with what we really want and with what we believe God wants for us. But if we intend to be obedient to God, to live in His presence, we must be willing to confront the misunderstanding of others and, if necessary, live with it.

THE IMPORTANCE OF BEING UNDERSTOOD

As a child Brian was different from his brothers and sisters. Deeply thoughtful and somewhat introverted, he was constantly the target of cruel teasing from his siblings and unreasonable pressure from his parents. He played the violin, guitar, and piano beautifully, but his father forced him to go out for football instead of taking music lessons. "Maybe it'll make a man out of him," his dad said.

Brian grew up confused about the value of his gifts and abilities. "Nothing I wanted to do was ever good enough for my father," he said. "I finally had to separate myself from my parents altogether in order to try to find out who I am. But it's hard not being understood by your own family."

Many of us struggle with the kind of conflict Brian faced. We feel that those closest around us—our families, churches, close friends—don't really understand who we are and why we make the choices we make. And we long for their understanding—and their approval.

The very fact that we have such a longing emphasizes a central principle of creation: "It is not good for the man to be alone" (Genesis 2:18). God's understanding of man's need for companionship, for a "mate," extends far beyond marriage into all the significant relationships of life. We need others; we need to feel connected to the world through meaningful interaction with other human beings. We need intimacy, and intimacy is founded upon understanding.

COMPULSIVE APPROVAL: A LIFE STORY

Terri was a "good little girl." She played nicely with her friends, never sassed her mother, and did what she was told. Early in life, she learned that she could avoid conflict and reap the rewards of praise and acceptance by conforming to the expectations of those around her. Throughout high school, Terri studied hard, obeyed the house rules, came in on time, and brought home friends her parents would approve of. Everybody marveled at the "perfect child"

Terri's parents had raised.

But the "perfect child" developed problems as an adult. Accustomed to approval, Terri had learned too well the techniques of keeping the peace. Approval to her meant love; when she faced difficult decisions, she made her choices on the basis of what others would accept.

When Terri became a Christian, she found that the patterns of compromise she had established as a child worked well in the church. She conformed; she took her signals from those around her and gained the approval of her "spiritual family" just as she had in the past—by not rocking the boat.

In the process of becoming what others expected her to be, Terri lost herself. She had no intimate communion with God, only an empty superstructure of acceptable behavior and the appearance of spiritual maturity. She was surrounded by superficial relationships. She was accepted on a surface level but not supported by real understanding. No one, not even Terri herself, knew who Terri was.

The desire for supportive approval is a strong motivator in human life. But the kind of approval that Terri sought— and that many of us seek—is not based on honesty but on appearances. We conform, we play the game, we live up to other people's expectations and standards, but the approval that we gain is hollow, for it is based on a false image rather than reality. When we fear misunderstanding so much that we will do anything for others' approval, our search for meaningful relationships degenerates into people-pleasing, compromise, and ultimately, a lifestyle of dishonesty.

THE INEVITABILITY OF MISUNDERSTANDING

When we live honestly and openly, allowing others to see beyond the surface into our struggles and questions, we are subject to misunderstanding. Inevitably, as we seek to obey God and make choices based on our understanding of His direction, we find ourselves at odds with others. But if we truly desire to walk in God's grace and live in harmony, we must take the risk of being misunderstood.

Because we live in an imperfect world, our relationships, our compassion for one another, and our understanding are also imperfect—sometimes painfully so. The pain connected to the misunderstanding we endure can be overwhelming, depending upon the level of misunderstanding we experience.

Daily choices. My business partner may not understand my decision to have crab legs rather than sirloin at dinner; my best friend may shake her head in dismay when she sees the wallpaper I have chosen for the bathroom. But these are relatively minor misunderstandings—they usually do not threaten my relationships, my security, or my self-image. I may try to explain why I like crab legs or plaid wallpaper, but whether or not others understand is of little consequence. The minor choices we make in life rarely bring us into a crisis of misunderstanding. The critical issues usually run far deeper than such superficial disagreements.

Behavioral patterns. During the turbulent sixties, Amy, a white college freshman, met Darrel, a black youth worker in a church several hundred miles away. They became friends, spending time together when they could and writing letters when they were apart. Amy's friendship with Darrel was quite innocent, but others—even her family—accused Amy of trying to "prove a point," using Darrel to make a political statement about civil rights. And no amount of explanation changed the minds of those who had judged Amy and Darrel.

Behavior—the choice of what we *do*—is a visible, external sign to those around us. And visible signs are often subject to misunderstanding, because "man looks at the outward appearance, but the LORD looks at the heart" (1 Samuel 16:7). When we judge others by what they do or fail to do, we miss the most important element of righteous judgment—the motivation, the "why." The judgment that comes by looking at outward appearances often results in profound misunderstanding and hurt.

Character. An even deeper hurt springs out of a more significant kind of misunderstanding: the inaccurate appraisal of a person's character. When someone misinterprets my behavior, I may be able to rectify the conflict through explanation. But when my character is attacked, I have no recourse to clear myself. Saying, "No, I'm not like that," when my character is unjustly assaulted—either by word or attitude—usually fails to result in any satisfactory changes.

Misunderstanding of character strikes at the deepest core of a person's self-respect—the inner soul of the individual. We want most desperately to rectify these misunderstandings, to change other's attitudes about us, and to put a halt to the attacks that can literally destroy the life within. But often these are the most difficult misunderstandings to confront—partially because people who go so far as to attack another's character often don't want to be confused with the facts.

Sometimes Christians honestly disagree about God's will. At other times, within the family of God, petty jealousies and bitterness spring up, causing division and misunderstanding. Sometimes anger and unforgiveness hinder understanding and acceptance. Whatever the cause, the judgment that is brought against a person's character results in untold damage to the individual, to his work, family, and relationships, and to his attitudes toward the church.

Brian nearly had his life undermined by such an assault on his character. Several years ago, he was involved in a shady business deal that included minor tax evasion. He had repented, confessed, repaid the money he owed, and started over, living honestly ever since. But his present lifestyle wasn't sufficient for Kay, the self-appointed righteousness guardian for the local church. She called Brian's new boss to let him know about his employee's indiscretion, "just for Brian's sake," so that he wouldn't be tempted to cheat again.

When a person's character is attacked, the wound strikes deeply, often causing irreparable damage and lasting scars. Forgiveness can help heal the hurt, but the misunderstanding that ensues can break fellowship and result in lasting division. Fortunately for Brian, his employer knew of Brian's mistake and trusted the changes he had seen in Brian's character. But Kay's sharp tongue undermined Brian's reputation at his church, and eventually Brian was forced to seek a different fellowship where he could worship and minister without being haunted by the specter of a past mistake.

One word of warning is in order: Living with misunderstanding does not mean condoning sin. If I persist in sin, claiming that "people malign me because they don't understand," I am not being true either to myself, to others, or to the Word of God. The confrontation of sin demands repentance, confession, forgiveness, and where necessary and appropriate, reparation. Misunderstanding, on the other hand, occurs when I truly seek the Lord, make my decisions based on His Word, but am nevertheless undermined by those who feel my choice is wrong.

THE VICTIM: GAINING PERSPECTIVE

Jill found herself struggling with misunderstanding when she made a decision unacceptable to her Christian friends. She had developed a friendship with Mandy, an unbeliever who seemed hungry for spiritual truth and open to Jill's sharing about Christ.

Jill's friends confronted her. "You can't keep spending time with Mandy," they insisted. "She's immoral—she's been into drugs, and everybody knows about the relationships she's had. She'll ruin your reputation."

Even though Mandy was unconventional, Jill had seen no evidence that there was any truth to the accusations. And if the rumors were true, that was even more reason for Jill to befriend her—Mandy needed the truth of the gospel. Jill cared deeply about her friend. Convinced that God had called her to this friendship and that she had done nothing wrong, she continued to share her life—and her Lord—with Mandy.

Eventually Jill became a victim of guilt by association. Rather than supporting her efforts to love Mandy into the Kingdom of God, Jill's Christian friends stopped associating with her, assuming—and telling others—that Jill had fallen away from her faith in Christ.

This story is not an unusual one. In every generation, Christians determined to do right have faced misunderstanding—even outright persecution—from others who disagree with their choices and judge them to be in disobedience. The Scripture speaks clearly to such judgment: "Who are you to judge someone else's servant? To his own master he stands or falls. And he will stand, for the Lord is able to make him stand" (Romans 14:4). Despite this warning, Christians far too often judge one another in ignorance, rather than supporting and encouraging God's individual work in and through each believer.

When misunderstanding that cannot be rectified by explanation arises, how can we call God's grace into the situation? How can we learn to live with misunderstanding in peace, without allowing it to destroy us?

Declaring independence. "If I were still trying to please men," Paul says in Galatians 1:10, "I would not be a servant of Christ." Paul was a man subject to misunderstanding, persecution, and unjust accusations both within the Church and without. Yet he said confidently, "I care very little if I am judged by you or by any human court. . . . It is the Lord who judges me" (1 Corinthians 4:3-4).

Paul knew the value of healthy independence—freedom from the compulsion to please others, freedom to stand before God alone. Such independence is not rebellion, the "I don't care what anybody thinks" attitude; nor is it isolation from others' responses or resistance to authority. Healthy independence is a recognition of a believer's unique call to serve God first and the willingness to stand alone, if necessary, to obey Him.

Independence is an unpopular term among Christians; it smacks of "Lone Ranger" theology, lawlessness, insurrection. But most of us are far too dependent—not upon God, but upon the approval of others. We take our signals from one another, we conform to arbitrary standards and derive our value and self-esteem from the approbation of our peers.

Melody Beattie, author of *Co-dependent No More*, warns against the dangers of trying to figure out what other people expect of us. "Don't worry about what others are thinking," she counsels. "Do what you need to do. If they're upset, you'll know it soon enough."[1]

If we want to serve God and to be obedient to His directions, if we want to have the strength to face the misunderstanding of those around us, we need first to declare our independence—not to separate from our brothers and sisters in Christ, but to distance ourselves from the influence of everyone else's opinion. Obedience to Christ is not a democratic action where popular vote rules; it is a deliberate decision to serve the Lord first, despite the misunderstanding of others.

Finding focus. The balance to declaring independence, of course, is establishing dependence upon God. Independence alone breeds rebellion; the important thing is not turning my back on other people's opinions, but turning my face toward Christ. The principle is one of focus: If I constantly focus on what other people think and how they respond, I put myself in the center ring of a circus, juggling for the crowds, trying to please everyone. If I concentrate instead on the voice of the Spirit as He directs me, the crowds fade into the background, and His will becomes the controlling factor in my choices.

"We are not trying to please men but God, who tests our hearts," Paul declared in 1 Thessalonians 2:4. Sometimes when we please God, others are pleased as well; sometimes those around us applaud our obedience. But when they do not agree with us, we are faced with a decision: to please God or to please man.

When we set our hearts to be obedient, no matter what opposition we encounter, we can rest in the knowledge of pleasing Him. God's grace upholds us as we do His will, and even when others misunderstand, we can enjoy the pleasure of His fellowship and the security of His presence.

Extending grace. Those on the receiving end of misunderstanding face two great temptations: spiritual superiority and self-righteous anger. But just as we wish to receive grace for the difficult task of living with misunderstanding, so we need to extend it to those who—either innocently or deliberately—malign our behavior and character.

Stephanie, who had chosen to obey God in reconciling a severed relationship, suffered grave injustice and isolation at the hands of her Christian friends. Yet she was able not only to receive God's grace in the restoration of the friendship, but to live in that grace on a daily basis and offer it to her tormentors as well. "I can't change their attitudes," she said, "but I can entrust them to God. I believe that what I've chosen to do is right, but I'm willing to change if God shows me a different course. Only God can reach their hearts and deal with their bitterness. Meanwhile, I can continue to love them and pray for them."

Stephanie's attitude demonstrates the healing power of God's grace to those who have been hurt by misunderstanding. If I follow the Lord's leading in spite of others' opposition, I may have to live with the pain of isolation and strained relationships. But if I focus upon God, sincerely seeking to do His will, if I am willing to follow His direction and extend His forgiving grace to those who have hurt me, I can live in peace whether I am understood or not.

A VIEW FROM THE OTHER SIDE

A compassionate young pastor with a bright future in ministry announces that he and his wife have agreed to a divorce. A beloved youth leader, suspected of inappropriate relationships with members of his high school ministry team, commits suicide on the day he is scheduled to meet with the church board. A college freshman, a leader in her congregation's singles ministry, becomes pregnant and has an abortion. A bright seminary student tests positive for AIDS.

Life throws us a lot of curves—situations we don't

understand, circumstances that seem to force us into judgments about the sins and choices of those around us, often those we love and respect.

How can we, who find ourselves on the other side of judgment and misunderstanding, respond with grace to the hurts and needs of others? Can we support the standards commanded by the Word of God and yet give strength to those who need it so desperately? Can we avoid inflicting the pain of misunderstanding upon others when we truly do not understand?

Jesus, in His encounter with the woman caught in adultery (John 8:2-11), responded in a manner that confounded the Pharisees but provides an imitable example for those who call themselves Christians. He said little during the episode, addressing one brief comment to the accusers and one to the accused. To the accusers He said, "If any one of you is without sin, let him be the first to throw a stone at her" (verse 7). To the woman He said, "Neither do I condemn you. . . . Go now and leave your life of sin" (verse 11). When we are faced with situations that foster misunderstanding, we can follow similar principles.

Remember your fallibility. "There, but for the grace of God, go I" is not a motto of superiority, but of humility. We are all capable of the worst sin we can imagine, and when we recognize—truly, deeply, at the essence of our being— our own fallibility, we are less likely to cast stones at those whose sin is not our own.

Look beyond the obvious. None of us knows what circumstances lie beneath the surface, what pressures and temptations another person faces, what struggles have gone on, unseen to all but God. Only He is capable of judgment, for only He can see the heart.

Keep silent. Gossip, the most treacherous and well-accepted sin among Christians, has the power to destroy relationships, careers, homes, and lives. "The tongue," says James, "is a fire, a world of evil among the parts of the body. It corrupts the whole person, sets the whole course of his life on fire, and is itself set on fire by hell" (James 3:6). Rumor is a match lit to the kerosene of self-righteousness; it destroys everything in its path. The Christian who wants to live by grace refuses to listen to rumor and keeps silent.

Have faith in the future. When Jesus told the adulteress to go and sin no more, He expressed faith in her. He did not excuse her sin or condone her actions; He said, in effect, "Put your past behind you and go on." When we are faced with situations that cause us to mistrust those around us, we need to have faith in God, in His redeeming grace. We need to place others in His hand and trust Him to do what needs to be done. Whenever possible, we need to express that confidence to the one who is torn by accusation and misunderstanding.

TWO FACES OF GRACE

When we face a crisis of misunderstanding—no minor disagreement, but a major, life-shattering accusation—we are placed in a position to receive an abundant measure of the grace of God. God understands—He knows our motives, our alternatives, our reasons, our choices. Although we would never choose to be embroiled in the conflict, the conflict itself is a place of refining, of purifying. We are forced to choose between pleasing God and pleasing others.

When we choose to please God despite the misunderstanding—even hostility—of those whose respect and approval we covet, we draw closer to our Lord, focusing upon His will and His direction. Swimming upstream can be exhausting, but it builds strength, and in that strength we can reach out in grace and acceptance to those who oppose us.

When those around us—our friends and loved ones, brothers and sisters in the Body of Christ—make choices we do not understand, we are in a different way called to a deeper experience of grace. We can extricate ourselves from the rumor mill, believe the best, and trust in God's ability to make the necessary changes.

Conflict may be inevitable, but we do not have to live in the stress of that conflict. Through grace, both the accused and the observer can live in peace—a peace derived from focus on God rather than circumstances, a peace that allows us to stand firm amid misunderstanding. The grace to be misunderstood extends both ways.

CHAPTER EIGHT

Suffering: When We Have No Heart to Pray

*What you thought you came for
Is only a shell, a husk of meaning
From which the purpose breaks only
when it is fulfilled
If at all. Either you had no purpose
Or the purpose is beyond the end
you figured
And is altered in fulfillment.*
T. S. ELIOT

M adeleine L'Engle, in *Walking on Water: Reflections on Faith and Art,* repeats her son-in-law's story of a beloved old Hassidic rabbi confronted by one of his youthful disciples. "I love you, my master!" the youth said.

The ancient teacher looked up from his books and asked his fervent disciple, "Do you know what hurts me, my son?"
The young man was puzzled. Composing himself, he stuttered, "I don't understand your question, Rabbi. I am trying to tell you how much you mean to me, and you confuse me with irrelevant questions."

"My question is neither confusing nor irrelevant," rejoined the rabbi. "For if you do not know what hurts me, how can you truly love me?"[1]

The reality of suffering is a universal principle of human life. We may try to escape it, seek to ignore it, or battle against it, but for all of us, life brings pain. The old rabbi's wisdom points to an important truth: If we want to love one another, to receive God's grace and support and extend it to one another, we need to recognize and identify the hurt that each of us faces.

The Bible is clear in its declaration that we should not expect to be exempt from pain. Paul informed Timothy that all who want to live godly lives will suffer persecution (2 Timothy 3:12). Paul himself suffered physical afflictions, imprisonment, and beatings and lived all his life with a torment that was never taken away (2 Corinthians 11:23-28, 12:7-10). Jesus, according to Hebrews 5:8, learned obedience to His Father through the things that He suffered. And as much as we want to be obedient, we wish—and often expect—that there could be another way.

A PERSPECTIVE ON PAIN

All of us are called to some measure of suffering. Some people, it seems, are destined to a deeper level of pain than others—catastrophic physical handicaps, incurable illness, deep emotional anguish. For such people, the significance of suffering takes on a different dimension, a level of importance that can be all-consuming. Others live with pain that is not so visible, but nevertheless viable—the loss of a loved one through death or divorce, the trauma of serious financial problems, the terror that comes during those dark nights experienced in our soul when we face ourselves and come to grips with our own sin.

Whatever the nature or intensity, each of us faces our own measure of suffering. Each person's pain is important, significant. While my struggle with personal relationships may pale in comparison with another's heartbreak in divorce, the hurt I face is still very real, affecting me profoundly whether I am aware of its impact or not. We all suffer; and to all sufferers, the word of God's grace speaks, responding to the universal, often unspoken, questions in our hearts.

WHY, GOD?

"Never, *never* ask God 'Why?'" a conference speaker once said. "God is not obligated to tell you why. Ask what you can learn from this experience, or how you can use this experience to help someone else. But don't ask God, 'Why?'"

The speaker reinforced a concept I had heard before: that we have no right to ask God why He did something, or—which is more common—why He did not intervene to stop tragedy or suffering or death.

God sometimes does not give us a direct answer to the question, "Why?" Sometimes He only reveals the "why" to us over many years of experience or insight; sometimes we never understand at all. But I don't believe that God is necessarily threatened or offended by my asking the question. Whether I verbalize the question or not, if it rises in my mind when things go wrong, when someone I love suffers, when life won't seem to come together, then I should talk to Him about it. God knows our hearts; He hears our unspoken questions. In Scripture, God gives some answers—perhaps not specific responses to our circumstances, but general principles that can guide our understanding about the "why" of suffering—and the "why not."

What did I do to deserve this? Many well-meaning Christians respond to the suffering of others by asking a common but condemning question: "Is there any unconfessed sin in your life?" The Bible is clear on the "laws of sowing and reaping" (see Galatians 6:7-10); we inevitably live with the results of the sinful acts we indulge in. But this principle of the harvest is a statement of fact, not a divine threat. God does not intimidate us with promises of impending retribution to incite us to holiness. He disciplines us so that we may share in His holiness, but He does not lash out at us with sickness or tragedy as punishment for violation of His law.

Perhaps the most appalling example of this misunderstanding of the "why" of suffering is evident in some Christians' response to the AIDS crisis. With little compassion for the victims of this ravaging disease, many people have proclaimed—quite loudly—that AIDS is God's judgment on the homosexual lifestyle, and that, in essence, such people deserve what they're getting.

These are not words of grace. This is not the response of a loving, compassionate Christ who no doubt would walk into hospital wards, fearlessly touching those whose family and friends have ceased to reach out. Many who have contracted this disease are reaping the natural harvest of a sinful lifestyle. Thousands of others—hemophiliacs, spouses, newborns—are the innocent victims of a worldwide epidemic. Whatever the cause, God reaches out, embracing, loving, weeping for the pain of His people.

Certainly we need to give attention to our souls; when sin is evident, we need to confess and turn from it. But we do not need to labor under a burden of guilt, thinking that God gives us unbearable suffering as penance.

If God loves me, why did this happen to me? Parents— even parents who love their children and are deeply committed to them—cannot always prevent their offspring from experiencing pain. Knees get scraped, bones break, a child's kidney disease requires surgery. The parents would undoubtedly take the pain if they could or substitute for their child on the operating table. But life doesn't work that way. Each of us, from the weakest to the strongest, must measure out the portion of our own suffering.

Christ, of course, took the greater part of our pain; He died for the penalty of our sins so that we could live eternally. As Paul declared in Romans 5:8, "God demonstrates his own love for us in this: While we were still sinners, Christ died for us." *God loves us*—there is no "if" about it. He demonstrated His love in the most graphic way possible: by sending His own Son to die so that we could live. And He did it while we were still alienated from Him, unable—and unwilling—to acknowledge or appreciate the price He paid.

Unfortunately, we often allow circumstances to control our interpretation of God's character, rather than letting the truth of His character dictate how we view our circumstances. We look at the pain, at the suffering, at the struggle, and we say, "If God is loving, He wouldn't let this happen." We forget what we *know* and rely on what we *see.*

God does love us. And as we focus on the grace of God, on His character, we can say instead, "God is loving, and therefore He can bring good out of this situation." Our understanding of the "why" may vary, but God's love, His grace, and His acceptance of us are constants upon which we can depend.

Who's in charge here, anyway? "Sickness is from the Enemy," Earl declared as we prepared to pray for Belinda's eye infection during our small group Bible study. "We should rebuke Satan and rebuke that infection, and she'll be healed."

Earl meant well. But like many other people in the Body of Christ, he had some unscriptural misconceptions about illness and the Bible's command to pray for the sick. Many Christians firmly believe that Satan has control in the world and in their lives. Their concept of spiritual warfare is a constant battle to exorcise evil from their circle of influence. Thus they give a great deal of time, attention, and emotional energy to the Devil, as if they were singlehandedly responsible for keeping him under control. And like ridding an old house of cockroaches, sometimes it seems to be a losing battle.

The Bible certainly supports the truth that the Church of Jesus Christ is in warfare—intensive combat against a powerful, invisible, personal Enemy. But sometimes we give Satan far too much credit; as one pastor commented, "The devil gets blamed for a lot of things he never thought about doing." Some illness, pain, and suffering relates directly to sinful choices. Some, perhaps, is a direct result of demonic activity—a reality that many more evangelicals are having to reckon with. And in general, all sickness, death, and pain are derived from Satan as the results of his temptation and the Fall.

But routinely to attribute all individual experiences of pain and tragedy to the specific work of the Devil is to bypass the larger issues of suffering, to opt for the "easy answer," the "formulaic prayer." And those who take such an approach often ignore the heart and emotions of the sufferer in their fervent determination to get the problem fixed and get on with life.

Scripture does show Jesus rebuking evil spirits in order to set people free from sickness and oppression.[2] On one occasion, He rebuked the illness itself.[3] But at other times He simply touched the suffering, or spoke words of compassion and healing to them. And whatever else we can identify about Jesus' technique for ministering to people, we see that He had no formula—only a love for people and a dependence upon His heavenly Father's grace.

The first chapter of the book of Job—the saga of a righteous man's suffering—presents a clear picture of God's control in the universe. Here Satan *asks permission* to bring suffering to Job to prove that he will not remain faithful to God. God grants His permission, but gives Satan only limited power.

Similarly, in *Paradise Lost* Milton portrays Satan as being totally powerless; he can do nothing except by the permission of God. Such insight helps us grapple with the issue of power and authority in a world that often seems out of control. God's purposes, as T.S. Eliot says, "are beyond the end you figured"[4]—our Father is in control of our circumstances, and the power wielded by our Enemy is limited and temporary. God's in charge here, and we can entrust ourselves to Him.

What in the world is going on? In this question lies the answer. "*In this world* you will have trouble," Jesus told His disciples (John 16:33, emphasis added). It was not a threat, but a simple statement of fact.

We live in a world racked by sin, torn apart by selfishness and greed. And as much as we might want to believe otherwise, one result of the fallenness of our universe is the presence of pain—physical illness and handicap, death, separation, emotional and mental trauma.

Far too often the church neither faces nor preaches that reality. Larry Crabb, author of *Inside Out*, comments,

> Modern Christianity, in dramatic reversal of its biblical form, promises to relieve the pain of living in a fallen world. The message, whether it's from fundamental-

ists requiring us to live by a favored set of rules or from charismatics urging a deeper surrender to the Spirit's power, is too often the same: The promise of bliss is for NOW! Complete satisfaction can be ours this side of Heaven. . . .

The effect of such teaching is to blunt the painful reality of what it's like to live as part of an imperfect, and sometimes evil, community.[5]

When we dare to ask "Why?" the answer we receive sheds only a dim light and gives only partial understanding. We suffer not because we are worthless people or, necessarily, because we have sinned. We groan because all creation groans; the unfair, undeserved, unbearable pain we feel and see around us stems from the unfair, undeserved, unwise choice of disobedience that plunged our race into darkness. We stumble because our world is fallen.

HOW CAN I ENDURE?

Acknowledging the reality and inevitability of suffering is only the beginning. Responding to God's grace in the midst of our pain—and supporting another sufferer with that grace—involves more than simply accepting that the pain is real and inescapable. Once the "Why?" has been confronted, we are faced with the "How?" How can I endure this unendurable experience? How can I find hope in the midst of hopelessness? And if I am not the sufferer, but the sufferer's loved one, how can I reach out in tenderness and acceptance?

From my youth, I was always a fixer, an action person. When a problem arose, I figured out and implemented the solution. That approach worked fine with household repairs and vacation plans. But when I applied it to humans in pain—including myself—the result was often disastrous. My heart was in the right place: I didn't want to see people I loved hurting. But the "hurry up and get better" attitude that I communicated did more harm than good.

If pain is a reality in human life, I cannot wish or force or ignore it away. Suffering must be reckoned with and, in the final analysis, lived with. To live with suffering gracefully, we must commit our struggle to the Lord and recognize that only He has the power to free us from pain and the wisdom to know if that liberation is in our best interests. In the meantime, we need to be gentle with one another—and with ourselves.

Walter Wangerin, in *The Orphean Passages*, describes the response of one woman to her suffering. Her husband's death plunges her into hopelessness, and those around her do not know how to respond to her despair. Wangerin's exhortation to the comforters speaks to us all:

> Do not cease to love her now; and surely never separate yourself from her.
>
> She hasn't stopped loving Jesus. That is precisely the conflict and the anguish in her. Loving is the pain in her, because her loving's unrequited. Soon enough this difficult knowledge will surface. . . . And she shall change again.
>
> Until then, love her. Honor her for the depth of her suffering, if for nothing else. . . .
>
> Be silent, as you are with all who mourn.
> But be near.[6]

When we suffer, or when someone we love suffers, appropriating the grace of God may be a difficult task. We need to focus upon God, upon His love and compassion, and recognize that God is not the source of our pain. Pain is a terrible reality of the world in which we live; our Lord, who lived in our pain and took upon Himself the ultimate agony of death, understands and weeps with us.

Grace in the life of one who suffers is not necessarily marked by a testimony of overcoming power. The smiling victory of the brave and suffering soul is not always possible—nor is it always realistic. Those who suffer may have no heart to pray, no desire for fellowship, no peace in the midst of turmoil. But God's grace supports us even when we cannot comprehend it. He holds us up with invisible hands, never letting us go, waiting patiently until the time when we can see Him once again.

When we suffer vicariously with those we love, God's grace gives strength as well. Jesus suffered for and with us, and His life gives us a pattern for sharing the sufferings of others. "Who sinned, this man or his parents, that he was born blind?" the disciples asked (John 9:2).

"Neither this man nor his parents sinned," said Jesus, "but this happened so that the work of God might be displayed in his life" (verse 3). Jesus did not condemn or blame; He reached out and touched, quietly showing compassion and love. And as we reach out to those who hurt, waiting in silence, holding out the hand of love and acceptance, the work of God can be displayed through us in healing love.

WHERE CAN I FIND SUPPORT?

The first rule of military service, a Vietnam veteran once told me, is "*Never volunteer for anything.*" The army of God often seems to operate on that principle, for our churches overflow with people who don't want to commit themselves—especially when commitment means the possibility of pain.

As a result, many suffering individuals in the Body of Christ find their pain multiplied by the burden of isolation. People at church are friendly enough, inviting them to the potluck dinner and the Friday night bowling party. But when the fellowship deepens beyond the level of superficiality, many Christians back off, unwilling to get involved in someone else's problems.

Stephen and Melissa struggled with just such a problem. Stephen, a recovering alcoholic, eagerly committed himself to his church's small group nurturing program. He hoped to find support and a place where he could be real and gain acceptance and encouragement. But it didn't work out that way.

"The people in the group, even the leaders, seemed to avoid the real issues of life," Stephen explained. "They wanted to seem open, so they shared a certain level of experience. But they were uncomfortable with me; they didn't want to hear about my pain, my struggles with alcoholism. They couldn't handle a problem they had no solution for; they wanted a quick fix so they would feel better. But the problems in my life aren't subject to a fast prayer and a pat answer."

Ultimately, Stephen abandoned the group. I understand his frustration; I, too, have experienced the disappointment that accompanies that kind of misunderstanding. But I also identify with those in Stephen's group. Dealing with, understanding, and accepting the difficult problems of life is not a simple matter of saying the right words. Many of us—myself included—have little experience in responding graciously to the unfixable problems and unanswerable questions of those we love. Baffled, we grope for comforting words or remain stoically silent; rarely do we succeed in communicating how much we truly care.

Helen Hanson, in her article "Open Arms for Wounded

Hearts," gives guidance to those who long to be supportive to a friend in despair. Reflecting on her own experience of facing incurable illness and the resulting hopelessness, she says,

> A compassionate response can encourage a person to endure in spite of his or her pain. It isn't necessary to have experienced the same kind of pain, nor does it require an in-depth knowledge of counseling. All it requires is that you care. . . .
>
> The lives of people are fragile and vulnerable. Our listening, touching, praying and loving may help restore a wounded heart and encourage a person to go on living.[7]

Hanson's directives provide not a formula, but a principle for giving comfort to people in pain. Those of us who do not experience the same kind of suffering cannot, strictly speaking, "understand" our friend's experience. But we can be there—sometimes in silence—offering love and acceptance. And as we extend the grace of compassion, perhaps we can help others respond to the greater grace offered by a God who does understand.

Paul, who knew what it was to suffer both physically and emotionally, speaks in Philippians 3:10 of his desire "to know Christ and . . . the fellowship of sharing in his sufferings." In Colossians 1:24, he refers to filling up "in my flesh what is still lacking in regard to Christ's afflictions, for the sake of his body, which is the church." As we enter into this "fellowship of suffering"—voluntarily committing ourselves in love to other members of the Body of Christ, we "carry each other's burdens, and in this way . . . fulfill the law of Christ" (Galatians 6:2)—the Lord's supreme command to love.

WHAT HAPPENS NOW?

Perhaps the consummate "Why?" question that arises regarding God's perspective on the nature of suffering relates to the purpose and outcome of suffering. As one man put it, "I can deal with almost anything if I know there's a reason for it. It's basically a trade-off: I'm willing to pay almost any price if I know the investment will be worth the dividends."

Paul realized that human pain and suffering accomplish important goals in the purposes of God. "Our present sufferings," he affirms in Romans 8:18, "are not worth comparing with the glory that will be revealed in us." And in Romans 5, he elaborates:

> We rejoice in the hope of the glory of God. Not only so, but we also rejoice in our sufferings, because we know that suffering produces perseverance; perseverance, character; and character, hope. And hope does not disappoint us, because God has poured out his love into our hearts by the Holy Spirit. (verses 2-5)

There are, the apostle knew, purposes "beyond the end [we] figured" in God's perspective of human suffering.

As we respond to struggles in our lives by casting ourselves upon the grace of God, we often find significant benefits: pain deepens us, softens us, causes us to grow in compassion and understanding, tenderizes our hearts, and mellows our harsh judgments and cruel condemnations. Second Corinthians 1:3-7 promises,

> The Father of compassion and the God of all comfort . . . comforts us in all our troubles, so that we can comfort those in any trouble with the comfort we

ourselves have received. . . . If we are distressed, it is
for your comfort and salvation. . . . Just as you share in
our sufferings, so also you share in our comfort.

Pain equips us for ministry. It tempers our character
and convinces us of the reality of the broken world we live
in. Suffering helps us understand the anguish of those
around us and gives us a glimpse of the sacrifice willingly
offered by Christ for our salvation and release.

WHO CARES?

There is perhaps no greater task the Christian faces than
truly embracing the grace of God in suffering. We are pro-
grammed by life, by society, by advertising to avoid pain and
seek out pleasure; we are taught, by precept and example,
that happiness and fulfillment are the greatest goals we
aim for.

The Bible gives us a different perspective. God, who
designs all things for our good, allows suffering in our lives.
We don't always know why; we are not always adept at
receiving our measure of suffering with a view toward God's
purposes. But whether our pain is temporary or constant in
duration, severe or moderate in intensity, of one thing we
can be certain: God loves us, and His tears are first to fall
when His children suffer.

CHAPTER NINE

Forgiving, Forgetting, and Forging Ahead

*If we cannot trust God to have dealt
effectively with our past, we may as
well throw in the sponge now and
have it over with. . . . But if God has
indeed pardoned and cleansed us,
then we should count it done
and waste no more time in
sterile lamentations.*

A. W. TOZER

A mid anger and accusation, a relationship breaks down.
First unconcerned and finally unfaithful, he has broken
his vows of fidelity. She sobs, "I can forgive you, but I can
never, never forget!"

A local church, once marked by loving service, is
ripped apart by strife over differing theology. A third of the
members leave, taking their bitterness and suspicion with
them to their new church home.

A Christian business falls apart, undermined by discord
as the company president systematically fires valuable
workers who disagree with him. Just as the company is
facing bankruptcy, the president leaves, taking on a position

of leadership with a competitor.

When at last the dust clears—in the marriage, in the church, in the business—appearances may be restored, but deep within, the gnawing cancer of unforgiveness grows, and the lives of many people are broken apart by unresolved bitterness.

Forgiveness is a primary teaching of the Scriptures. God promised redemption to Adam and Eve before they were banished from the garden; we await the ultimate fulfillment of that promise. Forgiveness is the gift of the Father's grace, offered to all who will accept.

But forgiveness doesn't end there. "How often do I have to forgive my brother?" Peter asked. "Seven times?"

"Not seven," the Lord Jesus replied. "Seventy times seven." (See Matthew 18:21-22.)

Forgiveness is a two-sided coin: My need to have my sins forgiven by the Lord is matched by my need to learn to forgive others. Forgiveness is a serious and sacred business, for the sin that precipitates the need to be forgiven is seriously unholy. Our sin sent Jesus to the cross; sin daily crucifies and tears apart His body on earth, the Church. If we wish to live in the grace of forgiveness, we must first face reality: the reality of sin's destructiveness, the reality of the restoring power of grace.

FORGIVE US OUR DEBTS

I saw the bumper sticker on the way to the office one morning: "*I owe, I owe, so off to work I go.*" The pun conjured up an image of seven whistling dwarfs, picks slung over their shoulders, tripping merrily through the woods toward their daily work in the mines. Most of us don't go to the mines so cheerfully—yet we owe, we owe, so off to work we go.

Sadly, we often transfer that perception of debt and work to our relationship with God. We are sinners in need of forgiveness—"we owe, we owe"—so off to work we go. We load ourselves with burdens of service to prove the seriousness of our commitment to God. We try to do better, to be better, to stop sinning and be righteous by sheer willpower. And we come home from the mines of self-effort, exhausted, sooty, and none the richer for all our digging.

Perhaps we need to change the lyrics of our refrain: "I owe, I owe, so to God's grace I go."

Indeed, we do owe ourselves to God. We have sinned; He has forgiven. We have needs; He supplies. But He forgives not because we are lovable, forgivable people, but because He is a loving, forgiving God. Forgiveness is based not on our nature, but on the Lord's.

EXPERIENCING GOD'S FORGIVENESS

"I resist acknowledging my sin," Nathan confessed. "And then when I do acknowledge it, I have trouble *feeling* forgiven. Once I face my sin, I don't feel worthy of forgiveness." Nathan expressed what many of us feel: Although we know intellectually the truth of God's forgiveness, we often have difficulty experiencing it in daily life. We carry great burdens of guilt and unresolved conflict, unaware—or unconvinced—that God's grace has made provision for our relief.

The interchange between Jesus and the "sinful woman" found in Luke provides some significant insights about the nature of repentance and forgiveness (Luke 7:36-50). Although there is no indication that a single word passed between the woman and the Master until the very end of the incident, her actions demonstrate several factors important in experiencing forgiveness.

Recognition of guilt. Modern popular psychology tells us that we "shouldn't feel guilty"—yet we *are* guilty, and acknowledgment of legitimate guilt is the first step toward forgiveness. "Godly sorrow," Paul says in 2 Corinthians 7:10, "brings repentance . . . and leaves no regret, but worldly sorrow brings death."

Too often we wallow in "worldly sorrow"—bad feelings, self-recrimination, low self-esteem. But none of these brings us into the reality of forgiveness. We can feel bad forever, but feeling bad doesn't accomplish forgiveness. True acknowledgment of guilt, true recognition of sin, takes the focus off our self-effort and places it where it belongs, on God's grace. We can never *feel* bad enough to atone for our own sins; we can never *be* bad enough to be beyond the reach of God's forgiveness.

Repentance. Having acknowledged her sin, the woman in Luke 7 took action. She did not make a resolution to stop sinning; she *came to Jesus.* Although forgiveness is never based on our own work or worthiness, repentance nevertheless is visible: a decision to change resulting in a turnabout in behavior.

When John the Baptist was preaching in the country around the Jordan river, he told the crowds, "Produce fruit in keeping with repentance" (Luke 3:8). We, too, need to demonstrate the fruit of our repentance—not righteous works earning forgiveness, but changed lives resulting from changed hearts.

Responsiveness. When Simon the Pharisee criticized the woman for her unseemly show of emotion (as we modern Pharisees often do to this day), Jesus took the opportunity to make a striking statement about the response generated by God's forgiveness by saying, "Her many sins have been forgiven—for she loved much. But he who has been forgiven little loves little" (Luke 7:47).

The implication of Jesus' statement—that great forgiveness results in a great response of love—sheds light on what it means to receive the forgiving grace of God. When we recognize our sin, we are overcome by a sense of our own unworthiness. In repentance we turn around, changing our direction—we come to Christ and lay our unworthiness at His feet. And as we receive His forgiveness, we respond in love and gratitude, recognizing that His grace, not our own righteousness, has set us free.

AS WE FORGIVE OUR DEBTORS

I had known Ron for several years—before his wife had an affair, before his divorce, before his commitment to Christ. I had watched him grow in faith despite incredible emotional stress, and our friendship had become a source of encouragement to me. As we had lunch, we talked about his job, his daughter, and his spiritual journey.

"The past three years have been really difficult," he admitted. "I thought my life was falling apart. But I'm beginning to learn what it means to be forgiven."

I might have said that Ron was learning how *to forgive*. In my estimation, he had been much wronged and had forgiven much. But his perception was different from mine. He saw how much God had forgiven him, and thus he was able to forgive those who had betrayed him.

Like the woman who anointed the Lord Jesus' feet, and like Ron, we grow in compassion, and thus in the ability to forgive others, as we grow in awareness of our own need to be forgiven. As we accept the grace of forgiveness, we are better equipped to extend that grace to others as well.

THE NECESSITY OF FORGIVENESS

Catherine had been hurt—deeply hurt—by a controlling mother and an indifferent father. After months of counseling, she finally identified the source of her long-buried anger, and after months of nursing that anger, she declared, "My counselor says I need to forgive Mother. But I can't—I won't—not until she realizes how wrong she was and apologizes."

Catherine had not yet learned an important lesson about the nature of forgiveness between humans: Forgiveness is a necessity, not an option, in the Christian life.

Forgiveness is necessary because God has forgiven us. When the disciples came to Jesus with the request, "Teach us to pray," He gave them a model for effective prayer that included the clause, "Forgive us our sins, for we also forgive everyone who sins against us" (Luke 11:4). This alarming condition attached to our own forgiveness leads us to conclude that forgiving others is a high priority in the sight of God.

In the parable of the unforgiving servant (Matthew 18:21-35), Jesus amplified the importance of forgiving others. The servant obviously did not value his master's forgiveness, for that forgiveness did not extend to the insignificant debt his fellow servant owed. Thus, as Jesus concluded in the parable, we must forgive one another *from the heart.* When we harbor unforgiveness, we fail to acknowledge either our need to be forgiven or the abounding grace of God freely given in Jesus Christ.

Forgiveness is necessary because it sets us free. Often we look too readily at the object of forgiveness—to the person who has wronged or betrayed us—as the focus of our forgiving. We want to get the crisis over with and come to a quick reconciliation. And often we mistakenly perceive that reconciliation is necessary for forgiveness. But as Catherine discovered in her conflict with her mother, sometimes reconciliation doesn't come readily—if it comes at all.

More realistic is a twofold perception of forgiveness: (1) I forgive those who have wronged me because Christ bought forgiveness for my wrongs; (2) I forgive others because I cannot have my spiritual and emotional life eaten away by festering unforgiveness.

Lewis Smedes, author of *Forgive and Forget,* emphasizes the necessity of forgiveness:

> Perhaps more to the point . . . is our need to forgive *for our own sakes.* Every human soul has a right to be free from hate, and we claim our rightful inheritance when we forgive.[1]

Forgiveness is a practical necessity, not a theoretical alternative.

THE PROCESS OF FORGIVENESS

"Maybe I do need to forgive my mother." After several more months of struggle, Catherine was growing in her understanding of the necessity of forgiveness. "Everybody tells me that forgiveness is an act of the will. But I don't know how to *will* myself to forgive; and even when I try, well, I just don't *feel* forgiving toward her."

Often we short-circuit the process of forgiving by attempting to forgive a deep hurt too quickly, too easily. Forgiving by the will is no quick fix, no easy answer to the problems of a hurt that needs to be healed. Just as we can trivialize God's grace in our own forgiveness by shortcutting the important steps of recognition and repentance of sin, so we can undermine the power of forgiveness in human relationships by saying "I forgive" without facing what needs forgiving.

Acknowledging hurt is the first step in the process of forgiveness. I cannot forgive a hurt I refuse to recognize; when I excuse it or ignore it, I block the path of true forgiveness. I may push the pain aside, but I have not dealt with it. The anger and resentment I feel festers beneath the surface, poisoning my spirit. If I intend to forgive, I must face the reality of the hurt I feel, even if understanding the hurt resurrects the pain.

When I clearly face the offense, I then must deal with my attitudes toward the one who has hurt me. The anger and resentment are brought to the surface, and I have a second choice: I can let the anger go, or I can nurture it into bitterness, recalling all the details of the offense. But before I can move past the anger, I must acknowledge it, saying in effect, "Yes, I have been wronged. I did not deserve to be treated this way."

Once recognized and confronted, my anger can be dealt with, and I can move on to the more positive aspects of forgiveness. In the third stage of forgiveness, God's grace comes into play: Gradually, as I admit my anger and choose to release it, I can begin to forgive the one who has offended me. As I decide to let my anger go, my feelings will follow—not immediately, perhaps, but eventually. And the one who has hurt me will no longer have control in my life. Rather than harboring bitterness, I can relax in the grace of forgiveness, entrusting the other person's attitudes and responses to God.

Movement through the first three stages of forgiveness is based on individual choice, a decision. I do not decide to be hurt, certainly—the hurt comes from another source, someone I have loved. Anger is a natural initial response to the hurt, but I can decide to face my resentment realistically. I can decide to choose to move toward healing rather than ongoing bitterness. I can forgive from the heart.

Beginning to forgive, of course, is often easier said than done. We need to deal with our feelings and honestly confront the intensity of the hurt. But we also need to place the betrayal we have experienced into perspective, recognizing our own capacity to betray and the depth of our betrayal of Christ Himself, who has extended forgiveness to us.

Forgiveness of another, like my own forgiveness from God, must always be based on honest confrontation and acknowledgment of sin. Neither excusing nor ignoring the wrong is true forgiveness. God never calls His people to dishonesty; He calls us to face reality and be obedient to Him.

My ability to forgive another, like God's forgiveness of me, is based on the reality of God's grace. But I must never demean the value of that forgiveness by saying, "It wasn't important, anyway." It *was* important—I was hurt, wronged, betrayed, sinned against. That is no trivial matter. My forgiving is no trivial matter, either—it **is the** "art of forgiving," "the miracle of healing."[2] Forgiveness is a sacramental act, an experience marked by God's presence and grace, a holy event.

We can forgive because we have been forgiven. We can show compassion and release our bitterness because we see our own sin and know our own capacity for evil. We can extend grace because we have received grace.

Jesus makes the principles of forgiveness irrefutably clear: We *always* forgive when we are wronged; we *always* seek forgiveness when we are in the wrong. We do not wait for someone else to make the first move; the one who inflicted the hurt may never acknowledge or confess the sin. But for our own health, our own freedom, and our own relationship with the Lord, we extend the grace of forgiveness.

REWRITING MEMORIES

"Forgive and forget," I once heard a speaker at a Bible conference say. "God forgets when He forgives, and we must, too. If you haven't forgotten, you haven't forgiven."

Nonsense! I thought. *Maybe God has the capacity of forgetting—after all, He's God. But I can't seem to forget. Even when I know I've forgiven, and when the hurts have been healed, I still have memories to contend with.*

Forgiveness and forgetting are not the same. Forgiveness faces the reality of sin and hurt head-on and deals with it in a godly way; forgetfulness often buries the pain under layers of superficiality and denies the need for forgiveness. Attempting to forget what has not yet really been forgiven only results in a festering cancer of bitterness and unresolved conflict. Lewis Smedes says, "If you forget, you will not forgive at all. . . . Forgetting, in fact, may be a dangerous way to escape the inner surgery of the heart that we call forgiving."[3]

We are conditioned by society at large and by our Christian subculture to avoid conflict at any cost. We are taught that the appearance of harmony is to be valued, that we ought not to risk confrontation, that it is virtue to let sleeping dogs lie.

But sleeping dogs do not lie still. The beasts gnaw away at us from within, poisoning our minds and destroying any remnant of inner peace. Unresolved hurt and unforgiven sin bare their teeth viciously, insistently. To be rendered powerless, sin must be forgiven. When true forgiveness takes place, we may still remember the hurt, but we remember it differently, without anger and resentment—instead, with understanding and the compassion born of grace.

DOES GOD FORGET?

Most of us in the Christian faith have been taught somewhere along the way that forgetting is essential to real forgiveness, that as God forgets our sin, we must forget the hurts inflicted upon us by those we have loved and trusted.

But does God forget? Psalm 103:12 describes God's forgiveness: "As far as the east is from the west, so far has he removed our transgressions from us." Isaiah and Jeremiah, in passages often used to support the premise that God forgets our sin, express similar ideas:

> "I, even I, am he who blots out your transgressions,
> for my own sake, and remembers your sins no more."
> (Isaiah 43:25)

> "They will all know me, from the least of them to the greatest," declares the LORD. "For I will forgive their wickedness and will remember their sins no more." (Jeremiah 31:34)

Perhaps the distinction is merely semantic, but there seems to be a subtle shading of difference between "forgetting" and "remembering no more." James Moffatt translates Jeremiah 31:34 as "their sin I never will recall."[4] An omniscient God cannot forget; He can, however, choose not to recall or bring to the forefront of memory sins that have been forgiven. He remembers without condemnation, and in His grace, He does not remind *us* of our former sins.

REMEMBERING WITH COMPASSION

"Be careful around Susan," a college friend warned me.

"Why?" I asked innocently. "She seems like a very nice person, and we have a lot in common."

"I've known her for two years," came the reply. "And she can be nice. But if you ever make a mistake with her, she'll never forget it—and she'll never let you forget it, either."

To my dismay, the warning proved all too true. I disappointed Susan once—I forgot a lunch date—and from that day on she treated me as if I were completely untrustworthy, reminding me at every opportunity of my unfaithfulness in forgetting our appointment. Susan had not learned the gentle art of compassionate remembering.

Having distorted the image of our omniscient Father, we humans are both blessed and cursed with memory. Often we forget what we'd like to remember and remember what we most want to forget. Seldom are we in consistent control of our thoughts and memories. Thus the painful remembrance of hurts we'd like to forgive and forget crowd our minds until we wonder if we'll ever be free and healed and whole.

While we can choose to forgive, we cannot so easily choose to forget. But we can make a different kind of choice regarding our memories: We can choose to remember with compassion rather than harboring unforgiveness. In biblical terms, we can bless rather than curse.

FORGING AHEAD

In the sweeping movie saga *The Mission*, former slave trader Roderigo has a stunning conversion after he kills his brother in a lovers' duel. He chooses his own penance:

carrying his armor, the symbol of his former life, in a death-defying climb up the mountains to the mission beyond the waterfall.

As the monks watch him staggering under his load, they can bear his pain no longer. One snatches up a knife and cuts the rope, sending Roderigo's armor crashing down the cliffs to the river's edge. In silence, but with a look of inexpressible suffering on his face, Roderigo makes his way slowly down the face of the mountain, retrieves his burden, and climbs painstakingly back up again.

"When will it end, Father?" asks one of the monks. "When will this penance be done?"

"It will be done when it is done," comes the reply. "Roderigo himself will know when it is done."

We do not, of course, have to do acts of penance in order to make ourselves acceptable to God and receive absolution. But we nevertheless should realize that, although forgiveness itself may come immediately, there may be an important time factor in our experience of that forgiveness. When we sin against God and then repent, He forgives us. Our reconciliation with God takes place immediately, although it may take some time to regain a sense of His presence. Our emotions often need the opportunity to catch up with the objective reality of forgiveness; we need time to let the dust settle and regain our perspective.

The ultimate goal of forgiveness is reconciliation. In human relationships demanding forgiveness, however, reconciliation is not guaranteed. It may come slowly, or it may never come at all.

Elizabeth struggled for years trying to reconcile a severed relationship between herself and her sister Mary Beth. But Mary Beth was not open to reconciliation; she harbored her anger and suppressed it until it was so well hidden that the rest of the family was sure that the trouble was over. Even Mary Beth believed it; she told others how the Lord had healed the hurts. But at family reunions and other situations demanding "forced fellowship," Mary Beth's anger inevitably surfaced in cutting remarks and icy indifference.

At last, Elizabeth realized that the relationship probably was never going to be reconciled. "I've done all I can," she concluded. "I've forgiven her, and I've asked forgiveness. I will always be open to reconciliation, but God must do that work in her."

Elizabeth discovered a truth that many well-meaning forgivers overlook: the first stages of forgiveness can be accomplished by one person alone; the final stage, reconciliation, can only be achieved by two. But lack of reconciliation, Smedes emphasizes, does not mean failure in forgiving:

> I think we can have reality even if we do not have the whole of it . . . forgiving can be real even though the person we forgive is out of our reach. We need not deny ourselves the healing of incomplete forgiving; we can forgive and be free in our own memories.[5]

When reconciliation is not possible—when our estranged loved one is emotionally out of reach, physically absent, even dead—we can nevertheless come to a satisfactory conclusion in forgiveness, put the hurt behind us, and get on with the business of living.

We can allow time for healing. Forgiveness is deep surgery, and mending takes time. We can forgive and be forgiven in good faith, but our emotions may still be raw and tender, our nerves frayed and sensitive. We must not expect instantaneous wellness; nor must we anticipate a smooth healing, free of scar tissue. We may always carry the marks of the wounds we have endured.

For the Christian leader, particularly, time for healing is essential. Whether he is the victim of another's betrayal or the perpetrator who has inflicted pain, the leader may need to step aside from his responsibilities to be alone with God, to confront his own need for forgiveness, and to work through his feelings about those who have hurt him. The individual soul is more important than the public ministry. We need to give God time to restore us and ourselves time to be restored.

We can make peace in the present. In Romans 12:18, Paul exhorts, "If it is possible, as far as it depends on you, live at peace with everyone." I rejoice in those "if" clauses, for they set me free from responsibility for another person's behavior. *If it is possible*, I will reconcile that broken relationship. *As far as it depends on me*, I will extend God's forgiving grace to others and live in peace.

We cannot control another's response in the process of forgiveness, but we can be obedient to God in what He commands us to do. We can choose to forgive and choose to color past memories with compassion. But where reconciliation is delayed or impossible, we must not allow an obsession with that relationship to rule our lives in the present. We must, rather, make peace with ourselves by responding to His grace, and we must hold in abeyance peace with that loved one—even if reconciliation is delayed until we stand before God's throne.

Forgiveness may be one of the most difficult lessons of grace, yet it is one of the most vital. As we learn to identify the Lord's grace in forgiveness, accept it, and extend that grace to others, we participate in a primary work of God's Spirit. And we become the tangible evidence of grace to those whom we graciously forgive.

CHAPTER TEN

Body Language

We don't go to church;
we are the church.
ERNEST SOUTHCOTT

Jesus told the story: A young man, full of his own desires and oblivious to his father's pain, took his inheritance and left home. After wasting his money on wine and women, reduced to working among the pigs, he came to his senses and decided to return to his father's home.

He had his repentance speech all planned, but he never got to give it. His father, watching for him every day, spied him on the road, ran to meet him, threw his arms out, and welcomed the prodigal home. (See Luke 15:11-32.)

A lovely story of grace and forgiveness had it ended there. But Jesus knew the human heart, its capacity for sin and bitterness. Enter the elder brother—angry, unforgiving, self-righteous, judgmental. "All my life I've worked like a slave for you," he complained. "And when this son of yours comes home after wasting everything, you take him back, no questions asked!"

In the parable, Jesus gives a realistic, if distressing, picture of the Church. Our heavenly Father forgives before the words of repentance are even spoken. Loving, accepting, restoring, He reaches out to the straying son and welcomes him back into favor.

But the Father has another son to concern himself with—the "good boy" who has stayed home and fulfilled his duty, but whose attitudes do not reflect those of his Father. The family, once divided by the prodigal son's flagrant sin, is now divided by the elder son's covert sin, a self-righteous indignation that he feels fully justified in maintaining.

We read the story, shaking our heads in dismay over the self-centeredness of the elder brother. We may throw in our lot with the prodigal, identifying with his headlong descent into sin and his restoration through the father's grace. But rarely do we admit that, just as we are all prodigals, so are we all elder brothers as well, wasting our inheritance by failing to take advantage of all our Father has given us.

The Bible describes the Church as a family, a body. And just as human families struggle with jealousy and bitterness, petty differences and critical separations, so the Church endures—sometimes in victory, often in defeat—the disputes inherent in human relationships. These are, as the title of Erma Bombeck's book suggests, "the ties that bind— and gag."

If we hope to live harmoniously as a family, a body, we need to learn both to accept grace for ourselves and to extend it to those around us. We need to identify the source of our divisions and attack them, rather than each other.

THE RUSH TO JUDGMENT

Barry found himself at the mercy of a merciless group of Christians. Because of the shady dealings of his business partners, he faced a very messy bankruptcy. His family was breaking under the strain, and Barry himself had developed a bleeding ulcer. When he brought his problem to the church, he was told that he must be in sin because things weren't going well. Had he prayed long enough before going into partnership with these swindlers? Why hadn't he heard God's voice more clearly? Didn't he trust the Lord? If he just had enough faith, his friends told him, God would get him out of this mess. If God didn't, well . . . the reason was obvious.

"The church," we are told, "is the only army on earth that shoots its walking wounded." The observation is a scathing commentary on the witness of the church in today's world. Yet we find these words all too true; congregations are divided and individual lives destroyed by the judgmental attitudes that fill our churches. We are very hard on one another.

The Bible, however, issues some stern warnings against irresponsible judgment. "Do not judge," Jesus said (Matthew 7:1-2), "or you too will be judged. For in the same way you judge others, you will be judged, and with the measure you use, it will be measured to you."

When I set myself up as judge of another person's life, I am saying, in effect, "I understand the situation. I have all the facts, and I am equipped to come to a conclusion about what is wrong here and what you should do about it." But I never really have "all the facts." The only way humans can judge is by looking at the external circumstances.

"Man looks at the outward appearance," God told Samuel concerning the choice of David as king (1 Samuel

16:7), "but the LORD looks at the heart." No matter how sensitive we wish to be, no matter how much we think we know, we can only judge from appearances. And Jesus said, in essence, "If you judge by appearances, you will be judged by that same standard." Chilling words, when appearances are so easily subject to misunderstanding and misinterpretation.

When I look at a fellow believer, I see where he is, what external manifestations of faith his life demonstrates. I do not see where he came from or how far he had to travel to get to this point in his faith. I cannot conceive of the emotional and spiritual hurdles he may have overcome or the maze of passages he wandered through in his exploration of faith. I cannot know the full impact of his background, the spiritual inheritance—or lack of it—that brought him to this place. I see only what is—and that I see only partially. God alone knows his heart, his motivations, his desires, his longings. God alone is equipped to judge.

SIMPLY SIN

Curt's parents sent him to Sunday school and church regularly. They never went, but they wanted their son to have some "religious training," so they faithfully dropped him off every Sunday morning. And just as regularly, they asked, "What did you learn at Sunday school?" (A question that deserves whatever answer is given!)

"The teacher talked about sin," Curt replied dutifully.

"And what did he say about sin?" the parents pressed.

Curt thought hard, trying to remember the gist of the lesson. Finally his furrowed brow cleared, and he declared victoriously, "He's against it."

We're all against it—at least when we see it in other people's lives. Sometimes we justify judgmental attitudes on the premise that "we cannot condone sin in our midst." Certainly God does not expect us to close our eyes to sin—the whole process of spiritual growth works to weed out sin and facilitate the planting of righteousness in our lives. But often we clothe ourselves in self-appointed right-eousness and wield the sword of truth against the sinners among us without regard to the individual lives we may be hacking to bits.

"Yeah, but Paul tells us to 'expel the wicked man from among you,'" Dave protested, quoting from 1 Corinthians 5:9-12. "He says not to associate with sinners and to judge those within the Body."

Dave was right, at least partially. Paul did indicate that we are not to tolerate flagrant sin in the church; in the case of the man who committed adultery with his father's wife, he called for a time of excommunication. But Paul's motives were clearly different from the motives we often have in judgment: "Hand this man over to Satan, so that the *sinful nature may be destroyed and his spirit saved* on the day of the Lord" (1 Corinthians 5:5, emphasis added). Paul was interested not in revenge, but in restoration.

And the story does not end with the man's excommu-nication—although sometimes we overlook or ignore the second act of the drama. In 2 Corinthians 2, probably written shortly after the first letter, Paul referred again to the inci-dent. Apparently the Corinthian church had obeyed Paul's instructions concerning the man, for in the second letter Paul had to tell them "enough is enough":

> The punishment inflicted on him by the majority is sufficient for him. Now instead, you ought to forgive and comfort him, so that he will not be overwhelmed by excessive sorrow. I urge you, therefore, to reaffirm your love for him. (2 Corinthians 2:6-8)

I once heard the story, told as true, of a man who was exposed in a sexually immoral liaison with another member of the same congregation. The man left the church, but after a while, he realized the depth of his sin and repented. In fear and trembling he returned to the congregation where he had been exposed, trying to slip in unnoticed.

But the elders had gotten wind of his return, and they were ready for him. When the service was over, they met him at the door *en masse*, embraced him in an enormous corporate hug, and led him out to the backyard, where a barbecue was prepared to celebrate his return. "We didn't have access to a fatted calf," one member explained, "but we figured a pig would do just as well!"

Those Christians understood the forgiving grace of God. Many of us would have roasted the sinner instead.

If we hope to learn how to extend grace to those around us, to demonstrate compassion and understanding within the Body of Christ, we need to recognize that our concept of sin is often quite different from the perspective of sin revealed in the Scriptures.

Sin is sin. We often operate according to an unspoken hierarchy of sin—a graph that ranks the seriousness of individual sins on a scale from one to ten. Certain sins, of course, are universally recognized as serious in their effect upon individuals and society: violence, murder, sexual infidelity, child abuse. Some actions, some irresponsible or evil choices, have far-reaching, even lifelong consequences both for the victim and the perpetrator.

No thinking person, Christian or nonChristian, would condone or excuse Hitler's genocide during World War II. No one makes light of murder or rape or violence in the streets. Our gradation of sin takes a much subtler form—we tend to excuse ourselves of our "little sins" on the grounds that those around us struggle with bigger, more serious problems.

But all sins, even the socially acceptable ones, have an effect upon the sinner and his relationship to God. All sin, in God's sight, is serious business: "Whoever keeps the whole law and yet stumbles at just one point is guilty of breaking all of it," James 2:10 says. "All have sinned and fall short of the glory of God," Paul emphasizes in Romans 3:23.

Although we give lip service to the principle, we really don't believe that sin is sin in God's eyes. After all, my negligent attitude toward God's Word is not nearly as serious as Joe's problem with lust. My tendency to interfere with other people's business can't possibly be as bad in God's sight as Laurie's divorce.

Yet until we realize that sin is sin, all of it repulsive to God and deserving of death, we will co-exist with one another in suspicion and backbiting, rather than living in love and forgiveness. My gossip or pride nailed Jesus to the cross as surely as Alan's unfaithfulness to his wife. When I look at *my* sin, at the depth of *my* struggle to respond in obedience to God, I can have greater compassion for others who struggle as well.

God's priority is restoration. "When someone sins against me," says author Walter Wangerin, "I have *rights of redress*—the legal right to satisfaction. Forgiveness begins when I abandon those rights, when restoration becomes more important to me than revenge."[1]

The church, however, often falls into the trap of seeking revenge. We don't call it that, of course—revenge is unspiritual! But like the elder brother, we want the returning prodigal to suffer a bit, to know the full depth of his sin, and to recognize the hurt he's caused. We don't want him restored too quickly—we don't, in short, want him to know the full measure of grace. We want him to pay for his sin.

But his sin is already paid for. And so is mine.

We are sinners—that is our human condition, a result of the Fall, an outcome of our original grandparents' disobedience. Our capacity for sin is infinite, unlimited—there is no sin I am incapable of committing. And if we wish to respond to the restoring work of the Holy Spirit in our own lives and draw the prodigals around us back into fellowship with the Father and His children, we must first be aware of our own sinfulness.

"If someone is caught in a sin," Paul instructs, "you who are spiritual should restore him gently. But watch yourself," the apostle warns, "or you also may be tempted" (Galatians 6:1). We are all subject to temptation. Remembering our individual and corporate weakness is the first step in communicating grace, acceptance, and love.

THE SIGNS OF GRACE

In the emotionally-charged movie *Children of a Lesser God*, a young deaf woman becomes romantically involved with a teacher in her school. The teacher, who both hears and speaks, tries desperately to get her to talk—he wants to hear her words as well as see her signs. She refuses—not because she cannot make the sounds necessary for speech, but because she rebels at his insistence that she enter into his world. She wants him to accept her as she is, on her terms, in her world of silence.

I do not know sign language well enough to understand all of it, but I am always struck by the expressive beauty of the language. Signs can often say what words cannot: the fierceness of anger, the futility of frustration, the embracing invitation of love.

Much of the communication of grace is, in a sense,

"sign language": nonverbal signals that convey forgiveness, acceptance, compassion, understanding. It is, in the truest sense, "body language"—the secondary message that communicates what is really in our hearts. And when our hearts are filled with the Father's attitudes, the silent signals of grace speak an eloquent language. Just as sign language carries a depth of meaning that cannot be equalled by the words it interprets, so—with or without the words—our loving responses speak hope to those who need to hear the message of grace.

I've been waiting; I hoped you'd come. When the father met his prodigal son on the road, he expressed not only his own hope, but confidence in his son's character. The boy had made bad choices and foolish decisions, but he was still his father's son. And his father was waiting, hoping, believing that his son would at last come home again.

I once became involved in some unbiblical teaching that drew me away from the church for a while. My pastor, a tender, loving man, had tried to talk with me about it, then finally fell silent and simply waited. After an eight-month absence, I sneaked into a Sunday service one bright spring morning—but I didn't get away with it. When I tried to sneak out the way I came, he was waiting for me. He grabbed me in a warm hug and whispered, "Welcome home. We missed you." He believed, and kept on believing, that I would come back to the truth.

You are welcome; you belong. The father met his son on the road not with a reprimand, but with an embrace. He reached out, pulled the boy to himself, and held him close. The son was where he ought to be—with his father. No matter what he had done, he belonged.

In the church today we are often reticent about embracing one another—both physically and emotionally. We keep our distance; we wait and see. Especially when someone we trusted has "backslidden," when a formerly faithful child has squandered his inheritance, we are quick to judge and slow to accept.

But those who are struggling with their own fallenness need to feel the reassuring touch of an accepting hand. They need physical embraces—hugs, an arm around the shoulders, the squeeze of a hand, eye contact, smiles, the holy kiss of fellowship. They need the intimacy of honest conversation, the sharing of a meal, an idea, a heart. They need acceptance.

When we prodigals come home, God does not "wait and see." He does not demand that we clean up our act before we come to Him. He embraces us, direct from the pigsty; the cleaning up takes place at home.

You will not get what you deserve. Neither the prodigal nor his elder brother got what he thought he deserved. The prodigal expected punishment—at the very least, to be treated as a servant. The elder brother thought he deserved more than his brother; his "faithfulness," he reasoned, merited him a higher place in his father's regard. But grace gives what we need, not what we earn—and God alone knows what our true needs are. Grace is a gift, not payment. As one of the angelic spirits says in C. S. Lewis's *The Great Divorce*, "Ask for the Bleeding Charity. Everything here is for the asking and nothing can be bought."[2]

When we look at ourselves and see the extent of our own fallenness, when we get close to others and smell the mire of the pigpen clinging to them, we realize how little we deserve forgiveness and restoration. Yet God does forgive, embrace, and restore. Even "if we are faithless, [God] will remain faithful, for he cannot disown himself" (2 Timothy 2:13). And He equips us, through an awareness of our own forgiveness, to reach out to others, extending to them not what they deserve, but what they need.

Seventeenth-century priest and poet George Herbert described man's experience of God's grace as light coming in through a stained-glass window:

> Lord, how can man preach thy eternall word?
>   He is a brittle crazie glasse:
> Yet in thy temple thou dost him afford
>   This glorious and transcendent place,
>   To be a window, through thy grace.[3]

The Christian is, indeed, a "brittle crazie glass"— broken pieces, painstakingly reconstructed to present an image of God to the world. The window may look like a jumble of cast-off scraps, but when the light shines through, the glorious plan of God is revealed in those broken shards of glass. None of us is exempt from brokenness, and none of us is beyond usefulness.

Performance is not the measure of your worth. When the father welcomed back his wandering son, he did not give the boy a list of expectations for his future behavior. Nor did he praise the elder son for staying at home and doing his duty. He summed up his priorities in a single line: "You are always with me, and everything I have is yours" (Luke 15:31). What was important to the father was not what his sons did—positive or negative—but who they were: they were *his sons*, and they were *with him*.

But many of us are members of the First Church of the Elder Brother. We are surrounded by comparisons of performance; those who "remain faithful" resent the restoration of those who have strayed, feeling somehow betrayed by grace. We need to hear and see and receive the signals of grace, the "body language" of acceptance. We need to accept the reality of our own prodigal natures, our own need for forgiveness.

Wangerin says, "I can forgive others only as I forget the one who has sinned against me and face Christ, against whom I have sinned infinitely, and who forgives me infinitely."[4] When we see ourselves as sinners, dependent upon the grace of God for our very lives, we will be gentler with the struggles of others, more compassionate, less condemning. In grace, we will be more likely to love and to leave the judging to God.

Perhaps the most gracious attitude that can ever be conveyed to a human being struggling with the reality of sinfulness is, "You do not have to perform. It's okay not to be okay." Accepting the individual does not mean condoning his sin, nor does it mean establishing his value according to the good things he does. It means acknowledging his worth as a person for whom Christ died, a gifted, valuable individual whose process toward Christlikeness is as important as the product.

We live in a graceless, unforgiving world. All we, like prodigals, go astray. When we come to our senses and turn toward home, we may be met not by a loving, forgiving Father, but by an elder brother holding a loaded shotgun. Or we may be elder brothers, unwilling to allow the prodigal's sin to stand forgiven.

Grace can interrupt the ambush.

CHAPTER ELEVEN

Final Focus

*God is an infinite circle whose center
is everywhere and whose
circumference is nowhere.*
AUGUSTINE

"I worry about accepting God's grace," a friend told me. "I want to live in grace and let go of my self-effort, but it seems—well, like grabbing at something I have no right to. I can't seem to receive grace and go on; somehow I think I need to wallow awhile in my pain, to give myself a chance to really feel the effects of my sin and struggle. Maybe only then do I feel that I'm worthy of His grace."

My friend's concern about "grabbing grace" too soon is a common response. We fear that accepting God's grace too readily trivializes sin and undermines the work of suffering and pain in our spiritual lives.

But responding to grace does not eliminate the need

for repentance; it only returns us more quickly to fellowship in the loving presence of our God. Brother Lawrence, "when he had failed in his duty . . . only confessed his fault, saying to God, 'I shall never do otherwise if You leave me to myself; it is You who must hinder my falling and mend what is amiss'. . . . After this he gave himself no further uneasiness about it."[1]

As we learn to focus upon God rather than upon the difficulties and struggles in our own lives, or upon our own ability to deal with our troubles, we recognize our inability to deal with our own struggles. We find that God alone is able to do what needs to be done, and we can depend upon Him to do it.

To receive grace readily is not to take God for granted or to minimize our own fallenness. It is, in fact, to acknowledge the depths to which we have fallen, to say, "I shall never do otherwise if You leave me to myself." It is the true humility that depends upon God alone.

The Bible teaches a principle of mutual exclusion. "No one can serve two masters," Jesus said (Matthew 6:24). "Out of the same mouth come praise and cursing," James declared. "My brothers, this should not be" (James 3:10). Likewise, we cannot focus our attention in two places at once. We cannot look at our circumstances and problems and also gaze upon the Lord's face. We must choose one or the other.

When we choose to wrest our attention away from the struggles that surround us and focus intently upon the Lord, our conflicts do not disappear. But they do fall into their proper perspective. Beyond the pain, beyond the misunderstanding, beyond the betrayal, we see the gracious, loving face of a Father who shares our sorrows and extends His grace to enable us to rise above them.

"My eyes are ever on the LORD," David declared in

Psalm 25:15, "for only he will release my feet from the snare." Caught in circumstances of conflict and snared in the net of affliction, David nevertheless looked *up* to the source of his redemption, rather than *down* to the source of his trouble.

Life is difficult; there are no easy answers. But there is a light in the darkness, a deeper reality than is evident on the surface. When we give ourselves over to the sustaining grace of God, like a wounded child relaxing in his father's arms, we experience the security and rest of knowing that He will, indeed, take care of us.

Our Father waits for us to lift our eyes, to focus our attention not on the snare at our feet but on the certainty of our rescue. And when we turn our attention to Him, He reaches out to us, welcoming us with His love and acceptance, embracing us with His grace.

Notes

CHAPTER ONE

Finding Focus

1. C. S. Lewis, *The Great Divorce* (New York: Macmillan Publishing Co., 1946), pages 33-34.

CHAPTER TWO

The Grace of Discipline

1. M. Scott Peck, *The Road Less Traveled* (New York: Simon & Schuster, 1978), page 15.

CHAPTER THREE

Failure: Turning the Curse into a Blessing

1. Madeleine L'Engle, *Walking on Water: Reflections on Faith and Art* (Wheaton, Ill.: Harold Shaw Publishers, 1982), page 46.
2. *The American Heritage Dictionary* (Boston: Houghton Mifflin Company, 1985), page 921.

CHAPTER FOUR

Balancing Priorities

1. Francois Fenelon, "Letters of Spiritual Counsel," in *Spiritual Disciplines*, ed. Sherwood Wirt (Westchester, Ill.: Crossway Books, 1983), pages 70-71.
2. Fenelon, page 72.

CHAPTER FIVE

Redefining Maturity

1. William Wordsworth, *Ode: Intimations of Immortality from Recollections of Early Childhood.*

CHAPTER SIX

Will the Real Me Please Stand Up!

1. T. S. Eliot, "The Love Song of J. Alfred Prufrock," in *T. S. Eliot: Selected Poems* (New York: Harcourt, Brace, & World, Inc., 1964), page 12.
2. C. S. Lewis, *Till We Have Faces* (Grand Rapids: William B. Eerdmans, 1976), page 294.

CHAPTER SEVEN

The Grace to Be Misunderstood

1. Melody Beattie, lecture given to Minnesota Christian Writers Guild, April 10, 1989.

CHAPTER EIGHT

Suffering: When We Have No Heart to Pray

1. Madeleine L'Engle, *Walking on Water: Reflections on Faith and Art* (Wheaton, Ill.: Harold Shaw Publishers, 1982), pages 70-71.
2. See Matthew 17:18, Mark 9:25, Luke 4:40-41, and Luke 9:42.
3. Luke 4:39.
4. T. S. Eliot, "Little Gidding" from *Four Quartets.*
5. Larry Crabb, *Inside Out* (Colorado Springs, Colo.: NavPress, 1988), pages 13-14.
6. Walter Wangerin, Jr., *The Orphean Passages* (San Francisco: Harper & Row, 1986), pages 105-106.
7. Helen Hanson, "Open Arms for Wounded Hearts," *Virtue* (October, 1987), pages 44-45.

CHAPTER NINE

Forgiving, Forgetting, and Forging Ahead

1. Lewis Smedes, *Forgive and Forget* (San Francisco: Harper & Row, 1984), page 20.
2. Smedes, pages 12, 14.
3. Smedes, pages 44-45.
4. *The Bible: A New Translation* by James Moffatt (New York: Harper & Row, 1954), page 863.
5. Smedes, page 36.

CHAPTER TEN

Body Language

1. Walter Wangerin, Jr., "Forgiveness," lecture given February 12, 1989, First Lutheran Church, Albert Lea, Minnesota.
2. C. S. Lewis, *The Great Divorce* (New York: Macmillan, 1946), page 34.
3. George Herbert, "The Windows," in *The Works of George Herbert* (London: Oxford University Press, 1941), page 67.
4. Wangerin, "Forgiveness."

CHAPTER ELEVEN

Final Focus

1. Brother Lawrence, *The Practice of the Presence of God* (Old Tappan, N. J.: Fleming H. Revell Company, 1958), pages 15-16.

P.O. Box

358

dodovus

Penn.

17311